I0037609

ADVANCE PRAISE FOR IGOR RYABENKIY

"Igor Ryabenkiy and I met when Miro was at the beginning of its journey. For a long time, he helped us as an advisor, participated in structuring rounds at an early stage, and later became one of our investors and a member of the board of directors. Now, Igor Ryabenkiy presents his book Adventures in Venture Capital, in which he shares his impressive entrepreneurial and investor experience which is sure to be useful to a wide range of entrepreneurs and venture capitalists."

-Andrey Khusid, Founder and CEO of Miro

"At the beginning of any entrepreneurial journey, it's important to surround yourself with knowledgeable advisors. While there are many advisors out there, not all of them are equally qualified. The truly valuable ones have a blend of knowledge and a sense of humor. Igor exemplifies this rare combination, and his book is a treasure trove of useful information presented in a relaxed and enjoyable way."

-Songe LaRon, Founder and CEO of Squire

Copyright © 2022 by Igor Ryabenkiy

All rights reserved.

No part of this book may be reproduced in any form or by any electronic or mechanical means, including information storage and retrieval systems, without written permission from the author, except for the use of brief quotations in a book review.

Illustration rights: Alpina Publisher, 2021

Illustrations: Marina Besfamilnaya

ISBN: 978-1-956955-51-4 (ebook)

ISBN: 978-1-956955-50-7 (paperback)

ISBN: 978-1-956955-61-3 (hardcover)

DISCLAIMER

This book contains only the author's personal opinion and his personal impression of certain events. In no event shall this book be considered financial, investment or any other professional advice. Investments are associated with significant risks, therefore prior to any investment, we recommend consulting with a professional.

Adventures In VENTURE CAPITAL

A Practical Guide for Novice Angels and Future Unicorns

IGOR RYABENKIY

LEGACY launch pad PUBLISHING

CONTENTS

GREETINGS AND HOW TO READ
THIS BOOK

This book begins with an autobiographical chapter that explains how I ended up where I am today. It is entirely optional, and you could just skip straight to the canon chapters.

There are two canon chapters. Both are pertinent, but the first speaks more to investors and the second to entrepreneurs. Feel free to read only what interests you—including the canons.

The choice is yours, but since there's a thin line between the two, I would recommend you read both.

You'll also find case studies at the end of this chapter that will be of interest to anyone involved in the venture capital process.

I hope you find it interesting!

PREFACE

MY PURPOSE AND INTENDED READERSHIP

Have you ever tried to answer the same question in an unconventional, interesting, fun and original way three times in a row? Ten times? Fifty? One hundred?

I have, and believe me, it's a special kind of torture. My profession requires that I frequently communicate with people —at conferences, seminars, negotiations and in interviews. Although the individuals are always different, the questions rarely vary. These are worthwhile and important questions, but as time goes on, I feel more and more like a trained parrot endlessly repeating the same talking points and truisms.

What's my line of work? In short, I'm what's called an "angel." No, I am not crazy. And to be more exact, I'm not an "angel," but more of an "archangel." Of course, I'm not referring to the heavens, but to the very earthly industry of venture capital investment.

An "angel" is a non-professional investor who invests money for their own pleasure. By contrast, an "archangel" (the highest rank among angels) is someone who invests in businesses professionally, combining private interest and the fulfillment of obligations to a venture fund, often one that they head.

My job is to find businesses that are just starting out, strive to turn them into "unicorns"—that is, market leaders worthy of a David Fincher film five years down the road—and then, of course, sell them.

For those who prefer numbers to metaphors, think of it this way: I am the founder and head of AltaIR Capital—an investment company with assets worth hundreds of millions of dollars—and am an investor with 25 years of experience, more than 150 companies in my portfolio and dozens of successful exits to my name.

To be honest, I never planned to write a book. The word "book" connotes something sublime and almost sacred, especially for someone raised on the classics. As I advanced in my professional pursuits, however, the very pragmatic need arose to put down in writing my answers to the questions I was most frequently asked. Of course, this is not an attempt to aggrandize myself or achieve literary distinction. I am an investor. My goal is both apparent and clear, and very much grounded in the reality of everyday life. My hope is that this small volume will help as many people as possible who are taking their first (or second, or third) step down the path of innovative entrepreneurship. I want to help them avoid the mistakes that I have made over the last 15 years. You can look at it as an entertaining guidebook through the obstacle course of those blunders. Naturally, you are bound to make your own missteps, but now you'll know where those hidden problems are most often found.

This book was born not from a momentary rush of inspiration, but from the frequent need to write down my thoughts during work, study and the process of preparing for public speeches and interviews. Some of those thoughts are included here, while others were left on the editing floor. Some I recalled only when transferring the contents of one computer hard drive to another, but all these fragments of thoughts long remained scattered and disjointed. Now, however, the time has come to synthesize them and turn them into proactive knowledge—the main tool by which this restless world constantly moves forward.

It is no exaggeration to say that I have extensive entrepreneurial and investment experience, and that the situations described in this book are based on real interactions with various businesses, entrepreneurs and managers, investors and angels, state officials and the members of development institutions in many countries.

For the skeptics reading, I would add that the path has not always been easy. Not only have I "spread my wings" as an angel investor and bestowed large checks on aspiring businesspeople, but I have also had to make major course corrections in life and have more than once lost everything, only to start again from scratch and succeed. In the process, I have learned the ropes of entrepreneurship and building a successful business. I know how to spot successful businesses early in their development and help them expand both financially and in expertise —and, of course, how to earn money in the process.

I own a number of profitable businesses and count dozens of successful startups among my investments. I have invaluable experience serving on the boards of directors of growing companies as well as the infrequent, but highly instructive, experience of working with businesses that utterly failed.

I don't consider myself some sort of guru, but I am often asked to talk about my experience in entrepreneurship and investing. I try to never decline such requests, even when I don't want to speak, because I believe you shouldn't be lazy if you can help even one person make their idea into a reality. Like any good entrepreneur, I want to maximize the effectiveness of these efforts, and writing a book is a good tool and a natural way to scale up my modest experience.

This book is not my only attempt to do something useful. I also participate regularly in the work of business accelerators and incubators around the world, and I teach and try in every way possible to assist those who want to learn and to achieve something. Now, the most important thing: this is not the sum total of my life and not my swan song. You don't see me making any retirement plans! AltaIR was growing and developing the whole time I was writing this book; deals were made, unicorns appeared and great exits happened. Yes, I like making money—not for the sake of counting it, but in order to go out and do things. With money, life is more interesting. Money is like fuel, and if you have somewhere you want to go, you need to refill the tank regularly.

To wrap up this long introduction, let me say a few words about how this book is structured. It consists of two main parts, with some lyrical digressions thrown in. The first part speaks to investors, the second to entrepreneurs. Although it might seem strange at first glance to bring advice to two such completely different types of readers under one cover, it would actually be stranger to separate them. For an investor to succeed in this industry, I am convinced that he or she must understand how an entrepreneur thinks, and vice versa.

No introduction would be complete without thanking those who helped make the book possible, and the following people have earned my sincerest gratitude:

-The AltaIR team, especially the investment and legal service teams. Thank you for working on hundreds of projects and for helping to resolve not only the usual but also the unusual conflicts that arose with startups and investments.

-My buddy investors and entrepreneurs who gave me valuable feedback on the book.

-Founders and teams of startups who let me have the knowledge I share here and who confirm the approaches in practice.

And to all my readers: may you find this book both useful and enjoyable!

MY INTRODUCTORY—AND PURELY OPTIONAL—AUTOBIOGRAPHICAL CHAPTER

This chapter is for those who would like to know how I got into venture capital investing. It also brings together the scattered bits of information about me that are circulating on the Internet.

I was born in Kazakhstan into an ordinary Jewish family of modest means. I spent all of my childhood and youth in Belarus, where I also completed my higher education. Because Jews had difficulty getting into the top universities in Moscow and Leningrad, I attended the Belarusian Institute of Railway Transport Engineers, where this discrimination was not an issue.

The name of the department where I studied included the word "telemechanics," and due to my ignorance of Greek, I assumed it had something to do with televisions. By my third year, however, it had become clear that telemechanics referred to remote control. One of the main skills I learned at university was building highly reliable systems. My thesis project was called "Management of the Moscow-Leningrad High-speed Railway." The authorities had wanted to build such a railway even back then, before Leningrad was renamed St. Petersburg.

Railways are notoriously risky affairs and history is full of bloody wrecks. For this reason, we were taught to develop comprehensive and foolproof systems that had multiple safeguards. Knowing how to assess risks correctly and account for a wide variety of factors that influence a situation is an incredibly useful skill in building railways, but as it turns out, it is equally useful in the venture capital investment business.

After graduating I moved to Murmansk, a far-flung city in eastern Russia near Finland. I worked for a time as an engineer at a design bureau. I was good at making RC circuits, but the other team members my age were far better as electrical engineers. I had to study like crazy while on the job in order to master programming and many other things. As a result, I became a highly sought-after systems programmer for our robots. At the same time, I studied automated control systems at Moscow Mining Institute's graduate school and seriously considered going into geological sciences

But 1986 was a crucial turning point for many of my peers because the authorities allowed people to open small businesses. I found this exciting, and started to look for possibilities to work in the emerging free economy. Soon, I already had my small team and they started to look and fulfill our first projects. It did not take long before I decided to concentrate on business, quitting my job as a programmer.

I started to work for an emerging IT company called Elecs, one of the most progressive IT market players at the time. Elecs expanded rapidly, and I began taking business trips to help develop a worldwide business structure.

The following year, Elecs moved its headquarters to Austria. The company's top managers (who had already made good money) soon left to start their own businesses, which freed up job openings for me and several other successful regional managers. However, a higher position in the company had one major drawback: it meant we would have to leave behind our well-established regional business. In the end, I was the only one who agreed to go. This turned out to be the right decision and had a positive effect on everything I did later because it exposed me to so many more facets of the business. We produced branded products such as computers, notebooks, floppy discs and peripherals—while also developing software.

Two years passed and the company continued to grow, branching out into new areas in addition to IT. The entire part of the business related to computers and software development was gradually put under my leadership, while the founders focused on a new area—banking. Our interests began to diverge: the Elecs owners grew less interested in computer development and I did not want to go into banking. In 1993, we opted for an amicable separation. My business partner and I had saved enough from our share of the profits to conduct a management buy-out and still have money left over to develop the business.

It also helped that I had developed good business relation-ships with business partners over the previous years, so they supported me with solid lines of credit. We created the Unit group of companies the same year, with me serving as presi-dent. It was headquartered in Vienna. Drawing on my prior corporate experience, I divided the company into several inde-pendent firms. The management of each firm received working capital and credit for participation. Speaking in the language of venture capital—the existence of which I still wouldn't know about for several years—we created several startups and engaged in their acceleration, albeit within a single corporation and under one leadership. Nevertheless, our managers had enough freedom to think of their projects as their own. As a result, we managed to grow several successful businesses.

I first tried my hand at pure venture capital investing in 1994. A strong team from St. Petersburg wanted to create one of Russia's first system integrators. I helped with the initial funding and was an active member of the board of directors for many years. The company quickly became a regional leader and then one of the most prominent players in Russia.

I liked that first experience with venture capital investing so much that I invested in a couple of other companies, also quite successfully.

Of course, I was caught up in the birth and development of the Internet along with everyone else. In 1998, I invested in Parallel Graphics, a leading virtual reality company at the time, and my investment helped the management arrange a buy-out from Silicon Graphics. My experience working with that company inspired me to start my own project and not to build on somebody else's existing business. I left my job as president of Unit in 1999, moved to New York and created the startup UnitSpace.

UnitSpace created online services at a time when comparable websites were only just appearing, and we actively participated in the work of pioneering international groups in this field. As a result, we were like a little bird that leaves the nest too early—the market was not ready to accept us. That was our first mistake. We were unable to build a scalable product, although we took pains to do so. Then the dot-com crisis in 2001 made a bad situation worse.

We failed to attract outside funding and our own funds began to dry up. Then, we made our second mistake as a startup: in a desperate search for our mission, we lost focus and started building custom systems for corporations.

This taught me one of the most important lessons, one that I will discuss in more detail later: even when faced with a lack of funding, a startup should remain focused on its main product and not get distracted with creating various services, no matter how attractive that option might appear.

Finally, we made our third and last mistake: we turned ourselves into a service company. This helped us earn enough money to stay afloat but prevented us from building a really scalable business.

I realized at that moment that I had gone down the wrong path. The whole enterprise had used up a great deal of time and had not led to the kind of success I had expected, though I was able to recoup my investment and earn a small profit, despite selling the startup for a nominal price. But more importantly, the missteps I made along the way proved to be a vital education in pitfalls and traps to avoid in all my future endeavors.

I quit Unit in 2005 and used the capital and projects remaining after the split to create AltaIR, a company for investment management. This was not a venture capital business in the strict sense, but more like passive portfolio investing. I bought small stakes in promising companies, monitored their growth from the outside and eventually sold them. I did not have to manage these businesses, apart from some mentoring. This lasted for several years before I decided that, although this was a good hobby that kept me fed, I would rather do something that actually required my participation. In 2010, I seriously considered becoming a university professor. "Why not?" I thought. "It's a great calling, it's also interesting and I have experience that is worth sharing with others."

In fact, I even had some teaching experience: In the early 2000s, I lectured on corporate entrepreneurship to the top students from some of the the best universities in Moscow. In 2005, I defended my doctoral thesis and became a Doctor of Business Administration.

Ultimately, life had other plans for me. It often happens that when you take a step in the wrong direction, fate gently takes hold of you and puts you on the right path. "Hello!" it says. "Haven't you figured it out yet? You're supposed to be over *here*."

As soon as I started thinking about teaching, then some former employees of my only moderately successful startup approached me for advice on projects that they had since launched on their own. I was happy to help and wound up investing in the project that later became Profi—a marketplace for professional services. Yegor Rudi, who had been one of the talented students in the course I taught, led the project. He introduced me to another project—LinguaLeo, in which I also decided to invest. This was about the time I discovered what is perhaps the best aspect of venture capital investment —the wonders of interacting with outstanding individuals. Over the course of selecting projects and working on them as they progress, I interact with a large number of entrepreneurs and specialists from all over the world. They are extremely passionate about their business ideas and many want to transform the world, or at least individual fields and industries. While I help them with my experience and knowledge, I gain even more experience, knowledge and energy from them.

By 2011, I began to get acclimated to the venture capital market and tried to find partners who could join me in identifying projects worth investing in. It is always better to work with someone who knows the territory better than you do and I have always liked working in teams.

But, I was not able to find professionals who were open to cooperation. In the end, I had to go it alone and overcome all the hurdles myself.

So, I did what I now advise novice investors to do as well: I allocated a manageable sum of money and tried to create a small portfolio of projects. That took a year and a half. Whether due to experience or luck, it turned out to be a very compelling portfolio. I quickly gained a reputation in the business community as a successful investor. This prompted the realization that it was time to begin investing professionally. It seemed as though this was what the universe wanted me to do. I put together a small team and began expanding the portfolio.

What is the difference between a professional market player and a non-professional? The same as between an alcoholic and someone who just likes to go out drinking on occasion. If the latter fellow feels like going out and getting drunk, he will; if he doesn't feel like it, he won't. The alcoholic, however, can't live without a drink. In other words, a non-professional player can create a portfolio, then sit back and relax. He has other things to occupy his time. What's more, his main occupation, whether a day job or business, usually generates income, part of which he can use to expand his portfolio. I used to be like that—an "occasional drinker." Now, as it turns out, I am a true "alcoholic."

At this point, I was fortunate enough to meet a remarkable and extremely successful entrepreneur who had a track record I admired, and soon after we met, AltaIR Capital (the proper name is AltaIR Capital, but Altair.vc is the website name) was founded in late 2012. This marked my transition from an angel who risks his own money to a managing partner whose profession is investing other peoples' money. This step carried a great deal of responsibility with it, and I took it only after some hesitation. That kind of responsibility is not something to take lightly. It seemed like only yesterday that I had been programming robots for a research project, and now I was managing the capital for startups to become great enterprises.

I started by putting together an initial portfolio of companies in Europe. Everything was going well, so I decided to try my hand at the global markets. I was well aware that the competition among investors was much stiffer and the sums involved were much larger at this level, but the potential earnings were also much greater, so over the next two years, we expanded our portfolio with projects from the two leading venture capital economies—the United States and Israel.

As a result, we invested the capital from our first vehicle in 18 months. Only a few projects really got off the ground, but those that did—such as Profi and Checkout—enabled us to recoup our investment. What's more, our sizable investments in US-based projects such as PandaDoc, SimplyInsured and Babylist grew significantly in value. PandaDoc later became our first official unicorn.

The time had come to transform into a serial management company. As a rule, successful venture capital managers create funds, invest the bulk of their capital in leading projects and then move on. Giants such as Andreessen Horowitz have dozens of funds; they can maintain a universal approach or adopt a geographic or thematic specialization. We launched our second fund in the summer of 2014. It started small but grew quickly, and within five years it had become quite large in terms of both price and assets. Our investments were very successful, enabling AltaIR to get involved in several projects that became global leaders in their respective fields, and to become a notable player in the venture capital industry. These included Miro, a project led by Andrey Khusid who created a platform for working collaboratively online in real time, a tool in demand for many millions of potential customers, including 80 percent of Fortune 100 companies. Another project in which we invested, Spot.IM (today OpenWeb)—the distributed social network created by Nadav Shoval—is now used by just about all of the world's leading publishers.

We also invested in Albert, the most popular mobile personal financial advisor, as well as the Joy app that helps tens of thousands of couples plan their weddings every month, and in the Hometalk project, an online platform for improving personal living spaces. The list goes on and on. Miro became our first decacorn in 2021. Later, Deel, a company that provides hiring and payments services for companies who employ international employees and contractors, became a decacorn as well.

Some of our more exotic ventures included investments in businesses based in India and South America, but none of these projects achieved any notable success. The lesson: before investing in a completely unfamiliar economy, you should study its national and cultural characteristics thoroughly. Otherwise, you aren't investing, but gambling. We will come back to this subject later.

We completed the initial investment phase of the second fund by mid-2019. Now, it focuses only on making additional investments and finalizing our participation in projects. We've made a large number of exits from projects and received a decent return on our investment, significantly exceeding the industry average.

We launched our third fund in 2020. It also focuses on early-stage projects, but in larger numbers and with larger average investments. We are actively working with talented teams and have already invested in several promising projects from Israel and the United States.

And we've immediately received some interesting results. Fast-growing fintech projects such as Lili and EquityBee showed 15 to 50 times growth in less than two years. Turing, a company that enables businesses to hire software engineers, became our first unicorn in this vehicle. Our fourth vehicle started in 2021, this time for late stage opportunities, and it is also growing despite difficult market conditions.

One great thing about the venture investment business is that it keeps you young. You cannot grow old because you are constantly starting up, and no matter what heights you reach, you can always state with confidence, "This is only the beginning!"

PART I

CANON FOR INVESTORS

1

HOW DO YOU KNOW YOU'RE AN ANGEL?

EARLY-STAGE INVESTMENT, OR: THE ART OF HAVING FUN WHILE LOSING MONEY

P remise:

You're at a party where you meet a young entrepreneur. Just one week ago, he came up with a brilliant idea for a startup but hasn't had a chance to tell anyone about it yet. You're the first. Right here, on a table napkin, he sketches an amazing technological solution that will turn the market upside down and make billionaires out of everyone involved. The young entrepreneur doesn't realize this yet, but your gut tells you it's true. You find yourself yanking your checkbook out of your pocket, flipping over the napkin and drawing up an *agreement by which you give the entrepreneur $100,000 to develop his idea in return for a share in the project.*

Question:

Does this make you a venture capitalist? Can you congratulate yourself and start giving TED talks?

Answer:

Not quite. Chances are that you just threw away $100,000—which means you should drink less at parties. But if everything does go well, if the young entrepreneur resists the temptation to buy himself a luxury Tesla the next day and actually goes on to create something worthwhile, then you can safely consider yourself an angel.

There is one simple and basic difference between business angels and the many other types of investors out there. The manager of an investment fund or company does this for a living, whereas a business angel does not. Angels also differ among themselves. Some know almost nothing about the field in which they are investing: they might have stumbled into the deal or are embarking on a small financial adventure for the first time. Others have some knowledge of the topic, but they invest as a pleasant and highly profitable hobby. Then there are "super angels" who are the top professionals in their field and invest their own money, making all of their financial activity a kind of private or individual initiative.

After all, everyone has moments when they get so excited they can't wait to go in on something crazy. Such a feeling sometimes overcomes me even now: I hear a tip from somewhere, my intuition tells me "This is the one!" and I rush to invest in someone's project. But when I give in to such an impulse, I risk only my own resources and never touch a penny of the fund's money.

For example, I recently got a call from an entrepreneur I know, and I ended up giving him a sizable personal check. I know he's successful, I understand his line of work and he explained everything to me in detail. So the deal went through quickly and without unnecessary delay—good for him and good for me. But it's not so simple for a professional investor who is responsible for other peoples' money. They must double-check everything and go over it in their mind a thousand times before taking a leap. A non-professional angel does it not only for the earnings but also for the satisfaction it brings. This does not mean that angel investments are somehow worse than professional investments and less financially promising. If you act wisely, angel investments can be very profitable.

Definition:

A business angel is a successful entrepreneur or manager who has surplus funds and the desire to use his or her experience and knowledge to help other projects—and to earn something extra, of course.

Twenty years ago, I didn't know what business angels were or what they did. I hadn't even heard those two words used together. But somebody later gave me a New Year's gift of a calendar showing a picture of me with wings on my back. That calendar turned out to be prophetic: in the late 2000s, I began investing in startups. It was then that I heard the term "angel investing" and realized I was doing just that. As I gained experience and made every possible mistake along the way, my approach to this hobby became increasingly serious. Now I am a professional investor. I have my own fund, a team, a number of projects in different countries and the burden of responsibility for the money that other people have invested. Sometimes the wings of that business angel inside me start to spread and begin lifting me off the ground an inch or two. In fact, this is also a prerequisite for success in the venture capital business: a professional investor should not take himself too seriously. As they say, "If you can't laugh at yourself, who can you laugh at?"

A Question from a Novice Angel:
Okay then, how does an angel become a professional? How is he reborn as an archangel and venture capital investor? Are their wings clipped, or what?

First, nobody has anything clipped or snipped. Everything happens naturally. You start out looking at a plethora of start-ups like a child in a candy shop. Everything looks so good to you that the first deal can happen very spontaneously and without any significant preparation. If you like it, you take it. Now you're an angel. But the moment you say, "No, I'm going to be choosier, I want to know more about how this technology works and have independent experts confirm that it really is what they say it is,"—as soon as that happens, you're reborn. Every potential project is now an object of research for you. You automatically move to another rank because you are becoming a professional.

What does this mean in practice? You hire a team and no longer approach the questions of risk and cost and revenue analysis as a non-professional would. You start building a completely different economic model—and the size of the check doesn't matter. I don't recall exactly when my endearing hobby came to include so many other people who are now also involved in the process. It's just that at some point you realize that you can't cope with the constant flood of information coming in, and so you think, "Well, I'll hire someone to help.

It's not a big deal. It doesn't cost much, and the payoff in terms of work accomplished will be significant." Then you realize you desperately need a financial expert. And then a lawyer. Next, you find yourself in an office packed wall-to-wall with staff. In no time at all, you've built a full-blown asset management company—welcome to your wonderful new world!

A "Bottom-Liner's" Awkward Question:

When an angel writes a check in the morning, he's counting on seeing the results that evening, right? But what if the entrepreneur can't deliver the goods? Does it lead to debtor's prison?

A check from a non-professional angel places a certain moral responsibility on the entrepreneur, but nothing more. It is obviously unpleasant to take money from someone and then screw up a project, ruin your reputation and crush your karma. However, that's about the extent of the risk involved if you're working with a civilized investor—and not someone with a bad attitude and brass knuckles.

When all the necessary documents are in order, the entrepreneur in whose project I invested should not only spend the money on the needs of the business until the next round of funding but should also keep me informed of his progress in some way. Nothing more is required. So, if the entrepreneur spends the investment funds unwisely and fails in their efforts, there is no administrative method by which I can force them to succeed. Therefore, the only realistic approach is to study the startup closely at the beginning and influence the project's team by working with it.

A Rule—or Rather, Several Rules:

I've made a lot of mistakes in my angel investments in startups and if I had a time machine, I would gladly go back with a list of simple commandments that, in my opinion, should guide any angel. We will refer to them in more detail later, but for now, let's just list them briefly and clearly, as on Mt. Sinai:

- Only invest funds that you can afford to lose.
- Invest only in projects that you understand.
- Don't chase hype.
- Invest in teams with which you feel comfortable working.
- Always write proper legal documents.
- Don't be a "backseat driver."
- Think from the very beginning about building up a portfolio of projects, and then gradually begin the process.
- Remember that you won't get your money until you exit the project.
- Know how to conduct a competent financial analysis.
- Don't forget about co-investment.

The Main Takeaway:

Not everyone should become a professional venture capital market player. But if you feel this is your calling, then go for it.

Again, keep in mind that for professional investors, this is:

1. The main line of work
2. The primary source of income
3. A full-time commitment and an ongoing process that requires a team of workers

For a non-professional, this is:

1. A pastime
2. A secondary source of income
3. Not necessarily a major time commitment

2

EXACTLY HOW MANY DOLLARS AND CENTS?

HOW MUCH SHOULD AN ANGEL INVEST IN A BUSINESS TO FACILITATE GROWTH AND NOT HINDER IT?

P *remise:*
     You've found a great startup. The technology is hot, the founders are pure gold and the team members, with a maniacal glint

in their eyes, are itching to get started. All you have to do is invest a small amount and then dig a huge pool for all the money you'll be swimming in. As for the size of your share, the founders, who don't have a penny to their name, say they don't care about such things and that you can take 100 percent if you want. All they care about is getting their project off the ground as soon as possible and seeing how far it can fly. It seems as though everything is perfect.

Question:

Is everything really perfect? What share will you take? If the founders have no ambitions in this regard and all they want to do is get their product to market, maybe you should just take the money and run with a 100 percent share. You've got the funds, nobody is opposed, and in a year's time the business will be worth a billion dollars. So what's the problem?

Answer:

The problem is that this is not, in fact, an angel investment—or any other type of investment. It is the purchase of a company with dubious prospects.

It has happened more than once in the history of aviation that a plane crashed after one of the pilot's friends or relatives stepped into the cockpit and tried their hand at steering. How does this apply to business?

Here is a typical situation that investors at all stages of the process must learn to recognize instinctively. A couple of "fallen angels" with sullied wings (you get the idea) decide to invest in Company X. They close the deal with a tough-guy handshake, saying, "To hell with a bunch of unnecessary formalities." And what happens next? A year later, these two angels approach the entrepreneur and put the question to him straight: "Dude, we gave you money, so where's the profit? You're a lousy manager, so either you start paying us interest or we'll take over ourselves. We'll figure out how to run this operation or else put this genius we know in charge." I know, I know —this sounds *weird*, but such things happen, so it is necessary to keep everything in clear legal constructions.

In such cases, I have only one question to investors who are so obsessed with "taking the helm": If you want to take control of the project and delve into every tiny detail of the company, what's the point of being an angel investor? Just go out and create your own company, hire anyone you want and run it yourself. These are two completely different pursuits: you're either an investor or an entrepreneur, but you can't be both.

You might think that investors only care about securing the largest share possible in promising new companies. That might be true of some investors, but my experience, and that of my most respected and successful colleagues, is that having a large stake in a project is one of the worst things that can happen to you. God forbid that I would ever again own anything larger than a 25 percent stake because every single time I have, things eventually devolved into an unhealthy parent-child relationship. If you exercise too much control over your child, you'll wind up with a weak-willed sniveler. It's the same with venture capital deals. An investor who greedily snatches up a major share falls into the trap of becoming overprotective. At some point, the employees of that startup—even if it's booming—will realize that they've been tricked, and this will inevitably affect the team's level of commitment. But most likely, such an enterprise will simply never take off because, having ceded all or most of their control, the startup's founders will soon lose their initial enthusiasm and turn into underproductive hired hands. I like strong, independent entrepreneurs. I help them achieve their goals, but I don't have to do their work for them because I don't have a large stake in the project and haven't left them with only a minority share.

The key here is the simple expression of "having more skin

in the game." If I am the only one "risking my skin" because I have the largest share, then I have more at stake and that makes me responsible. Accordingly, if the entrepreneur has invested nothing or very little, then what can they lose? It turns out that I am the one taking all the risks, while the entrepreneur simply found an eccentric fellow who gives him money. Is that good? This is how the psychology of a hired hand is formed, albeit one with a small share—and such businesses work very poorly.

Rule:

It's better to have 10 percent of a billion dollars than 100 percent of a million. A smart investor is not interested in getting the maximum share at the start, but in growing the business, together with its founders, as much as possible. And if the founder no longer feels that the project belongs to him, you can kiss all hope of success goodbye. Nothing will help. Game over.

Never ignore this rule!

Entrepreneurs are people of action—that's how they're made. Employees are no worse, of course, but they think differently. When an entrepreneur ceases to be responsible for every step he takes, the game becomes uninteresting to him, even if he himself doesn't realize this metamorphosis. He loses the very motivation that has been driving the project's progress. In effect, he is no longer an entrepreneur at that point. He understands that he has a wealthy and powerful friend who has invested a lot of money and owns the lion's share, and since the business belongs more to the investor than to the entrepreneur, the headache of running it should be his as well.

I have had projects fall prey to this mistake. In fact, I have one such project in my portfolio right now, although the situation is slowly (very slowly!) improving. The project is good, the idea is great and I like the entrepreneur—he is a strong individual and businessman. But after bankrolling the business for a year and a half as a pure angel investment, I got a letter from the entrepreneur saying, "Hey, we've run out of money."

"How did that happen?" I asked.

"Well, it just did. We need a loan."

"If you need a loan, then go to a bank," I said.

It's like the old anecdote:

A man sits on the steps of a bank and sells peanuts. An acquaintance approaches the peanut man and asks if he can lend him 100 dollars. The peanut man says, "I can't, as I have an agreement with the bank."

"What kind of agreement?" the acquaintance asks.

"Ah, simple. I do not lend money and they do not sell peanuts."

I have a firm rule in this regard: Banks don't sell peanuts, and I don't lend money.

Even the best and most intelligent founders often come down with the "Oh—we're out of money!" syndrome. This requires constant educational efforts to cure. In the situation mentioned above, I told the fellow, "Yes, I am a partner with deep pockets and yes, I am prepared to give you much more money than I have already invested. I like this project. But I don't want you to come to me acting as though it's my problem that you're out of money. You should have thought about it six months ago and planned your budget so that you wouldn't have to ask for more. If you saw that the need would arise, you should have convinced me in advance to invest more."

This is an extremely typical example. My share in this project is not very large, but imagine what would happen if I had the majority stake?

Some of these cases are merely routine. A startup submits a funds request even though no agreements were made to this effect, which results in a rejected request.

Some situations are just funny. One startup founder said she was losing her motivation because she couldn't pay herself a market salary. She demanded that the investors pay more—not to make the project more profitable but simply to increase her salary. Certainly, it did not work, and predictably, the startup didn't succeed.

Exception:

The opposite can also happen: a founder considers the business so much their own that, without even consulting the investor, they begin playing a risky game and wind up destroying a profitable project. They make reckless moves without listening to the opinion of their business partners. They rent a huge office, hire attractive assistants, lose control of the finances and even steal money directly from the project. All of this inevitably leads to a crash. If they had risked only their own capital, they would have been free to do whatever they wanted. But they forgot that they were in the same boat with others who were counting on the business to succeed.

Something like this happened to me once. I had a 16 percent share in a project. They hit bottom several times and each time came to me for funds. Then one time, the founder came to me saying, "Hey, we've got a cash gap. We urgently need a thousand dollars." I said, "This amount is nothing fatal. We can help, But I'd like to take a look at your books and see what's going on." I had previously taken his word for everything. In a few days, an audit revealed that they had a cash shortage of much more than forty thousand. The shortfall was even larger than my share in the business—and they didn't even realize it. They hadn't been trying to cheat me; they had simply been careless and made childish mistakes. In the end, the cash gap turned out to be 50 times more than the original figure they had named—and the project fell apart two weeks later.

The Main Takeaway:

If you are the first investor in a project, try to obtain a reasonable share, one that isn't so big it will dampen the team's motivation. Don't try to run the project yourself: that's what the founder and team are for.

If you are a co-investor, your concern should be for the pool of investors as a whole and not your specific share. The main objective is to have a harmonious relationship so that the business grows and provides for a successful exit.

3

HOW I INVEST: FOCUS

WHY BEING AN ANGEL IS THE BEST PROFESSION ON EARTH (AND POSSIBLY IN HEAVEN)

P *remise:*
  You have devoted half of your life to creating a variety of industrial robots and have done quite well, becoming a top specialist and earning good money. You've spent the second part of your life investing in startups that design and build robots for everyday and industrial use, and have also done well in this field. There were no get-rich-quick stories, but you generally came out ahead when exiting a business. Now a friend introduces you to a mysterious Vietnamese businessman who is looking for an investor. He seems trustworthy and has a good reputation, but there is one problem: his startup deals with processing rapeseed fields in Vietnam. There are

no robotic solutions involved whatsoever, only something about bioengineering and selection. The Vietnamese entrepreneur claims annual growth will reach approximately 700 percent. It sounds like a dream come true. But maybe it really is just a dream.

Question:

Growth at 700 percent?! It's simply incredible. Should you go for it?

Answer:

Probably not. Don't be greedy.

When most people think of a small, very professional venture capital fund, they imagine a roomful of analysts tirelessly searching the world for the most valuable new products and services. The job, they think, is part science, part journalism, part reconnaissance and part traveling salesman. The reality is very different. We do follow trends and look for new technological solutions in our area of interest, and we do have to look at a large number of projects in different countries, if for no other reason than to understand how things are developing in different places, but we spend most of our time looking at projects that are presented to us—that is, projects that have somehow found their way into our "inbox."

The fact is, although there are numerous such incoming projects, not all of them fit our profile. Perhaps the idea under consideration is truly brilliant but that industry is not for us. That is why the very first question I ask myself when considering a project is: "How much of this do I really understand?" If I have some understanding of the subject, then the next step is to study the market, get acquainted with the founder and his company, and gauge how ambitious they are. That's what I like doing, but most of the time I'm flooded with proposals for opening some café in India, or working with rapeseed fields in Vietnam. Applicants often promise the moon, but what if I can't tell Vietnamese rapeseed from an Indian birdseed? In other words, what if the business in question falls outside my area of expertise and I don't have a trustworthy individual who can guide the way? This leaves us no way forward, and even if we can find experts in the field, we prefer to stay within the limits of our sectoral and geographical expertise.

In rare cases, projects outside our chosen profile are so appealing that I decide to put down my own money as an angel investor, but I would never draw on the fund's resources for that.

As a rule, no sane investor would ever get involved in a project without having solid expertise in that field, so it is always important for a founder to be aware of who would want to invest in his project and why. After all, you go to a bakery for bread, not basketballs.

A Question from a Newly Minted Investor:

I have mastered only one thing in my life: how to make the ideal thread for a nut—and that's how I've made my fortune. And that's why my competence in the world of modern startups begins and ends there. However, I have money to spend and I am determined to become an investor. Where should I start?

Knowing how to make the perfect nut is nothing to sneeze at. It means you have good experience and just need to find the right industry for your investment. But investors who really want to spend money and lack broad experience are more likely to consider publicly traded companies. As a rule, closed, privately owned companies do not want outsiders to know much about them. For understandable reasons, they try to limit access to their internal workings, but as an investor, I need to know who and what I'm dealing with: I can hardly imagine making high-quality venture capital investments without having sufficient expertise and knowledge of the company in question.

Obviously, a human mind can hold only so much knowledge. Fortunately, I have an investment team composed of very talented and well-rounded people that greatly expand on what I could accomplish alone. I often listen to my staff, which has paid off well on many occasions. Still, even with the combined competencies of my investment fund members, choosing successful investments is still like navigating a minefield: the first step can go fine, but the second—KA-BOOM! Therefore, we have selected several areas in which to concentrate. For example, I know nothing about the space industry—who the players are, which technologies they use and which way the solar wind is blowing—so I don't invest in those things. In other words, we focus. With investing—and probably in life in general—focus is one of the most important things.

Axiom:

The grass really is green in many places, but you can't pursue projects in every attractive and resource-rich field out there, no matter how much you want to. You need to be able to focus on a particular industry, build up experience and develop a deeper, rather than broader understanding.

Rule:

An investor is not just a money bag with legs whose only job is to open up at the right moment and spew out gold coins. His main occupation is to learn new things constantly. To achieve success, he must be curious, read a lot, observe and talk to people. This is exactly what makes being an investor the best of all professions: you are surrounded by smart people—much smarter than you—from whom you are constantly learning.

And you earn money while you're doing it! Could anything be cooler than that?

The Main Takeaway:

Try to invest only in projects that you understand. At the early stage, intuition and gut instinct are even more important than analyzing financial flows and the current structure of the business. Investing at this stage is more difficult, but if you choose well, projects produce high profits with small investments.

The key to always following this rule is this: if you cannot explain the gist of the project to yourself in simple terms, the project is not for you.

4

HOW I INVEST: GEOGRAPHY AND MARKET

WHERE GLOBALIZATION ENDS AND REALITY BEGINS

Premise:
  Let's say that you are an investor living somewhere in Peru. You are approached by talented startup founders from the small African state of Resol that borders Rwanda and Somalia. You don't speak French and they don't know Spanish, but somehow, you

all manage to hit it off. The African businessmen want to address the shortage of drinking water in the region and have come up with an innovative way to extract potable water almost from thin air. It sounds like a good project that could not only earn you some money, but also land you a Nobel Peace Prize.

Question:

Has this mysterious and exotic startup piqued your interest?

Answer:

For starters, read the name of the country backward and think again. Next, a glance at the map will show you that Rwanda and Somalia are on different parts of the continent and have no common borders.

American investors once had a curious rule that I can fully appreciate: never invest money in a business that is more than 30 miles from your home. Why? The answer is simple: you could always drive there to see for yourself how things are going. Then you could discuss the details in the same language, without the difficulties of translation and cultural differences interfering.

Although globalization is gaining pace and the world is becoming more ordered and streamlined, all the best players I know in the venture capital market are not expanding but narrowing their focus. There seems to have been a great deal of truth to that old American saying. It might seem odd, but the greater the physical distance involved, the more tenuous the connection is, regardless of how many instant messenger apps you have on your smartphone.

For example, I once invested in a project based in New York that was doing just fine where it was. But one day, its founders went to Australia. That did it: something had clearly gone wrong with the project, and try as we would—and we tried every means legally available to us—we could not make it work again. Having learned this and similar lessons, we decided to narrow the geographic spread of our assets to North America, Israel, UK and some projects in Europe. That is, we chose countries that we could reach easily and where we wouldn't encounter cultural or language barriers.

Physical distance is only one factor affecting the investment market. Another, much more important aspect is scalability. And this is to say nothing of cultural considerations. It is very important to quickly silence your inner Know-It-All who thinks that just because they have traveled widely, they can understand other peoples and cultures overnight. Cultures differ widely: Japanese, Chinese, Arabic, Russian, Indian. You can talk all you want with residents of these countries and know the names of all their many presidents by heart, but you will always be something of a space alien there. An outsider. Only a deep and long exposure can give you a better understanding of the people in another country—and even this is no guarantee.

Many of our attempts to work in other markets eventually hit an unpleasant dead end owing to our ignorance of the finer points of local culture—on which much, if not all of the success of the projects depended. For example, at one point we decided to pursue a venture in Brazil—and not alone, but with an experienced Brazilian business partner. We had long, fruitful discussions in which we studied everything in detail. We received a realistic assessment of the project and could see no obstacles in our path. The investment required was not especially large, so we saw no reason not to give it a try.

The idea was to extend credit to pensioners and civil servants, in other words, people who receive nearly guaranteed regular payments from the state. However, it turned out that in Brazil, an extraordinary number of goods are counterfeited and this applies to documents as well, including documents proving a person's identity, employment status and financial solvency. As a result, we were overrun by requests for loans from people carrying fake and even stolen IDs, but we didn't realize it at first. I wasn't naïve, but the fact that the banking market was so poorly controlled in Rio came as a surprise to me. Without going into too much detail, I can say that we ran into some very wild stuff there. But despite the enormous scale of forgery and counterfeiting in Brazil, we hadn't taken even basic precautions.

In another instance, we decided to invest in what seemed to be a good project in India, a kind of marketplace for car repairs. The initial figures were promising. When the time came for a new round of funding and we began talking to the entrepreneurs about it, we suddenly learned that they were now doing something completely different from what we had agreed to. They had started by repairing cars, but by this time had switched to simply selling used cars. But why? Large and successful players were already operating in this niche and we had absolutely no advantages over them. The founders did not agree with our belief that it was more profitable to repair cars in India than to sell them, even though we had already invested in the idea. The business collapsed after a few months because the local team took too narrow a view: they were looking at the market from the perspective of local residents rather than considering the global dynamic. They had quickly conducted an experiment to expand the niche, and when it seemed successful, they hastily decided to revise the original plan and dive head and shoulders into the expanded niche. This is a common mistake: I know of several other projects—in which I did not invest—that met exactly the same end.

Rule:
A startup must position itself in a definite geographic location because it is important that investors are able to gauge whether it will be a local or a global market.

A project is ideal when it has a local focus but can scale up without any restrictions. That is, when we make a serious investment, we want the business to have global prospects, or at least a chance of becoming a dominant player in a major domestic market. To generate the desired financial return, a project must have a large potential market and the team must have an understanding of how to conquer that market.

A Skeptic's Objection:

How could you possibly know at the start whether something can be scaled up?

Just look at the market! Study it painstakingly and scrupulously and you won't screw up. Let's say you have Product X. What is your next step? You look at the customer segment, its characteristics and the percentage of people who could become regular customers. You also consider the strength of the competition and how your product is different. It is very important that you answer these questions honestly, considering every side of the question so that you can get a clear picture of the market. After that, you must determine what share of that market you can achieve. Of course, there is a fair bit of guesswork involved, but if you don't take this step, you are guaranteed to make numerous classic and painful mistakes.

For example, let's say some people came to me saying, "We plan to sell movie tickets online." I ask what value to place on the project. After some hesitation, they set it at $10 million. I say, "Okay, let's do the math." We start counting and it turns out that all the players in this market combined can earn only $30 million—and that is provided the market holds, which as COVID proved, it might not.

At this unpleasant realization, I say, "Well, fellas, it turns out that you don't have a market and your project couldn't have that value. Even if your project only cost $1 million, we would probably only consider it briefly before saying 'no.' With such a small market, it's a nonstarter. Nobody will ever buy a project aimed at such a limited segment."

At times, entrepreneurs are so mistaken about their capabilities and the project's scalability that it takes on Homeric proportions and becomes one of those comical instances when truth really is stranger than fiction. Consider the following incredible, yet typical situation. A man came to me quoting some very attractive numbers. He had calculated his possible annual returns but then mistakenly thought they were monthly instead, and so multiplied that figure by 12, making the project look truly amazing. I looked at the figures and said, "My friend, why did you multiply this number by 12—and two times at that?" The fellow was himself taken aback by his inattentiveness. And this is why we insist that everyone comes to us with a financial plan. It puts your thoughts in order and helps to avoid making irreversible mistakes.

Rule:

A lack of scalability can be due not only to a small market but also to one that is so fragmented it becomes unprofitable to reach customers and impossible to get them hooked on the product.

The issue of scalability proved to be the death knell of an otherwise very good project I once had. I financed it personally as an angel investor, and so I maintained a clear conscience before the fund. But we made a classic, even somewhat childish mistake.

A friend of mine decided to financially support a business his relative was starting and he came to me for advice. I decided to help my friend by giving him some seed money. Actually, this wasn't a purely selfless act: the idea for the business was pretty good, but the project ended up failing anyway. The relative who was founding the startup was a professional mover. He knew everything about the field, was thoroughly acquainted with the market and was planning to start a transportation business in the US for people who were relocating from one home or office to another. There was one crucial problem: moving was a highly targeted service that customers don't use very often. People relocate from one house or office to another only very rarely, so it is nearly impossible to predict, much less guarantee, whether customers will return. The founder decided to create a kind of national aggregator, a large online platform to which he then had to attract a lot of traffic. So, he spent the necessary funds, did the marketing, and began bringing in clients. Then he did some accounting and found that he had spent roughly $100 for each new client gained. The freight carriers that used his online platform charged $500 for their own service and paid a $100 commission to the platform for each gig. This meant that the initial cost of attracting a client was recovered from the very first job, and that each additional order would be pure profit.

It made perfect sense on paper. However, there was just one "but"—namely, that if these clients returned at all, they would not reappear more often than once every two or three years. A lot can change in that much time. People might start traveling by quadcopter or living full-time in the Metaverse by then. Despite the founder's efforts, it was impossible to ensure the amount of traffic and user return needed to create a well-coordinated and systematic demand for the service. All the clients moved just once, and that was the end of the story. And, because the project had many expenses in addition to the figures associated with the order itself, it experienced a growing deficit without any hope of shifting into the black. Thus, it was necessary to consider not only the return on the cost of attracting a client, but also how much time the client would spend with the project and what lifetime value (LTV) he would bring.

Many proposals sound good, but not all of them make money. As Karl Marx said, "Practice is the criterion of truth."

Objection from a Techno-Universalist:
You just need to create a universal product right from the start and look for an infinitely vast market. Then everything will be fine. Consider a messenger service, for example. What difference does it make in which country it works? And retention isn't an issue: if someone has already started using the service, they'll stay with it for a long time. And the costs are reasonable.

Objection to the Objection:
Creating a universal idea for an infinitely vast market is something out of the realm of science fiction. The market for instant messaging apps, for example, already has 20 major players—how would we elbow our way into that crowd? We would have to come up with some kind of 100 percent-guaranteed killer feature and then find a component that would make it go viral—or some other aspect that would compel billions of our fellow earthlings to use it.

And since we're talking about texting services, here is something else to consider. messaging apps come in two types: specialized and general. Specialized messengers focused on a single segment or topic of discussion. General messengers host overall topics for different types of communication. I've already had one unsuccessful experience in this field. A business partner and I invested a modest sum in a general messaging app. He invested a huge amount, but he asked me to join for my name—although he is not less well known. We put in our money and the whole thing went belly up almost instantly.

Despite the fact that we had a good product with lots of bells and whistles, it didn't have that certain something that could entice users away from the big name competition.

Making a general messenger app now is just as strange an idea as creating a social network, where you'd be going up against giants like Meta. And it would be a mistake to assume that if Meta has such a value, your product will, too. You should first understand who needs your product and why. For example, there is a social network specifically for families and it even has an artificial limit on the number of friends permitted. I can use WhatsApp to talk to anybody, but here I talk only to my loved ones and kin. The idea is clear: the Internet is too big.

There is a worldwide trend toward making the Internet less global and more localized. Many people are sick to death of everyone seeing everything they do. More and more, people want privacy and peace. Still, we didn't invest in this project for a very simple reason. Although it had a clear focus on the audience, it was very expensive to reach the subset of users we wanted. If we targeted everyone at once, then most users would simply be too lazy to install another app on their smartphones and figure out how it works. I already have 100 such messenger apps—if I download another, it will be the 101st, and all just to talk with my wife and kids? Why bother? I can just create a separate group in Whats-App for that.

I might be wrong sometimes and overlook what could have been a mega-hit. But as a rule, in deciding whether to invest money, we always look at the market volume and the cost of entering that market. At this stage, a huge number of ideas fall short already. Specialized messengers continue to emerge and we have successful investments in some of them.

A Rule—Or, Rather, a Summary:
If you enter other markets, it's best to work with someone

who knows that market, or else you should understand it yourself. If you are working in your own market, you are obligated to understand everything yourself. If you are the main or the only investor, you must stay in constant contact with the founder or else the day is not far off when your money will disappear somewhere. Personal meetings, online communication and constant monitoring of the project status will also help in this situation. It is also better to limit the geographic distances involved, but this is a matter of individual taste.

The Main Takeaway:

When choosing the geographic location of an investment project, you should be guided by your own experience, understanding and connections in those specific markets. In theory, you can learn the ins and outs of any market, but the more distant or unfamiliar it is, the greater the effort and focus it will require. Choose markets that "feel right."

5

HOW I INVEST: THE TEAM FACTOR

WHICH FOUNDERS ARE BEST KEPT AT ARM'S LENGTH

P *remise:*

Two wonderful founders of a promising startup come to meet you. You have no qualms about the business part of the negotiations: you see at once that they know what they're doing and understand their target market. But as the meeting continues, you notice one founder looking deeply at the other, who in turn occasionally gives his colleague a meaningful glance of reassurance. You realize that they arrived in the same car and use only the pronoun "we" when talking about the business. You don't have to be Sherlock

Holmes to understand they're in a romantic relationship, but as a tactful person, you don't ask questions about their personal life.

Question:

If your suspicions prove true and the founders are romantically involved without disclosing it, should you worry about the company's prospects? Or is your cynical heart so hardened that it simply resists everything beautiful on this earth and sounds the alarm in vain?

Answer:

The situation is definitely unsafe. Better to think it over very thoroughly first, and then multiply all of the risks by two.

To paraphrase Tolstoy, "Happy startups are all alike; every unhappy startup is unhappy in its own way." But founders create many of their problems themselves by establishing the wrong relationships among team members. *The Beatles* didn't split up because the world was fed up with the Liverpool foursome, but because once the band members reached adulthood, John, Paul, George and Ringo became so different from each other, they chose to go their separate ways. Of course, there is no universal formula for building a team, and any team can fall apart at any time and for any reason. After all, human relationships are fragile and tend to fray where the bonds are weakest. I have several stories from my personal work experience that prove this unhappy point.

One of the basic rules I try to observe is not to invest in a business in which the founders have something personal at stake. Parents and children, husbands and wives, brothers and sisters, sons-in-law and mothers-in-law, and lovers are all very risky. However unpleasant it is, it isn't unusual for business partners to split because they disagree about how to develop the business. But it is much worse when people split up not over business issues but because their mutual love has turned to mutual hatred: divorce, a father's anger or even a simple loss of shared affection almost always guarantee that an otherwise good project will fail.

When founders begin taking different approaches to the business, you can usually catch the signals in time and take prompt measures. But when everything seems to be going great one day, but comes grinding to a halt the next—and all because an undercurrent of negative emotions has grown so strong— that is an extremely painful and unpleasant experience.

We had such an experience once. It was a very promising project—cloud storage for photos that included a photo editor service, elements of a social network, the ability to create collages and many other nifty things. A husband and wife team created it. He was the hardcore tech guy and the brains behind it, while she was the heart and soul of the startup. Everything was so good and so beautiful that I fell in love with this company—something that, of course, an investor should never do. The business took off, expanding from a small audience to more than 2 million users in a single year. Microsoft offered us a grant for use of the servers and everything was coming together. But the more you grow, the more difficult every subsequent step becomes. Sensing their own lack of professional experience and trying to compensate for it, the founders began hiring new people. This started causing friction among the team members but the worst was yet to come.

One day, I learned that the wife had suddenly moved to New York to improve her English and write poetry. Just like that. Apparently, the heart had found a new lover and had dumped the body of our project. The husband also had some kind of romantic fling. He ran away—we later found him in Egypt—without paying for the servers. The project fell apart right before our eyes due to some incredibly stupid moves. In the end, Microsoft simply shut down our servers and the entire database was lost. This, by the way, is a good lesson for startups.

If you are offered a grant to use the cloud, don't forget to check the invoices. Once you've accepted the grant, you won't be able to bargain and you'll end up having to pay for the service at the highest rates.

The worst part was that prior to these problems, the project had been going strong: I considered it the third best in my portfolio and I had received a very good rating for it. I could have sold it for a good price right then, but I was blinded by "investor's infatuation" with the project. I wanted to make it even more outstanding, and this feeling was continually reinforced by the enthusiasm that my market colleagues expressed for the project. No one could believe that for such a relatively small sum it was possible to grow so much.

Rule:

Any company run by two individuals who are romantically involved is a major risk and you should make every effort to avoid getting involved with it. Of course, there are exceptions, but even those rare success stories will probably encounter serious problems at some point. The great majority of couple-run businesses fail.

I like to joke that, as with married founders, anything of a serial nature needs special attention. This next anecdote is a little less dramatic, but just as instructive. It concerns serial entrepreneurship.

People love to read about entrepreneurs who establish one successful business after another, selling each and then moving on to the next. They don't fixate on any one business their whole life, but confidently shift focus from one industry and economic model to another, easily parting with the fruits of their creativity. I respect serial entrepreneurship, but sometimes this phenomenon generates curious cases.

I once joined forces with a well-known serial entrepreneur,

investor and all-round active guy, in every sense of the word. He called me up and said, "Listen, there's this cool startup. It's a great idea. I'm going to jump onboard today and you're welcome to come along." He sent me the write-up, and I saw that it was only an idea at that point and nothing more, but even the bare-bones idea looked promising and even more so with Mr. Serial Entrepreneur attached to it. I decided to join.

The company took off, and one year later we were raking it in. Twelve months after that, he left the company and started a new project, inviting me once again to join. I was still flying high over how much we had made on the first one and figured we would hit the jackpot again. I liked this new idea as much as the first. We sat down to discuss it, and I said, "Listen, I'm ready to invest even more this time. Our first project together was an unknown for me. I just put my faith in you. But this project is in a field that I'm very familiar with and understand. I can take a position on the Board of Directors, and that way I'll be helping while you're doing the heavy lifting."

But Mr. Serial Entrepreneur did not get personally involved in the new project at all. He simply introduced me to four people whom he said were his team of founders. But these "founders" were more like figureheads who were hands-off and left strategy to groups of researchers who had no business acumen. Three months later, I announced that because my partners were not upholding their part of the bargain, I was pulling out. With that, we parted ways, and two months later, the project quietly ground to a halt. Strange as it might sound, I experienced both my quickest success and my quickest failure while working with the very same serial entrepreneur.

Rule:

A serial entrepreneur is no more likely to succeed than

anyone else is. You need to work just as carefully and be just as exacting with them as with all the others.

Serial entrepreneurship is an uncertain thing. It often happens that an entrepreneur fails repeatedly, but gets great PR. He could create the public image of a successful person, but if you dig deeper, you find that everyone he's done business with has only lost money. And it might be that he really does create successful businesses, but after he sells them, they somehow fall apart just as quickly.

Why is it that the public and even many investors love listening to serial entrepreneurs—in stadiums filled with paying attendees, on YouTube channels and even in their own offices? It all comes down to a simple psychological phenomenon: for some reason, we are certain that if a person has walked a tightrope between two skyscrapers once, he doesn't need any special preparation to do it a second time. You might be surprised to learn that some serial entrepreneurs are terrible businesspeople and that only by some miracle have they managed to avoid falling off the tightrope and into the abyss. In fact, I've gotten burned just as often by serial entrepreneurs as by startup teams with little experience.

So, how can you tell which teams are good and which are not? While there is no magic formula for success, you can always make sure that each of the founders brings something substantial to the project and that it doesn't all rest on the shoulders of a single genius. Although it isn't obligatory, it is usually better if one team member is a technician, another manages the business side of things and a third does the marketing. The team must be competent, open to the outside world and have a strong entrepreneurial spirit.

I also look for teams whose members I like. On several occasions, I invested in projects with whose founders I found it difficult to communicate right from the start, which is always a red flag. Once, I put such concerns aside and invested in a business that I understood but that was started by someone whom I found inscrutable. And in the end, nothing came of that project.

A proverb sums this up perfectly: "Better to argue with a wise man than agree with a fool." I have always tried to follow this principle. You and the team should be like-minded individuals to some extent, or at least be able to communicate freely with each other for the sake of your common interest.

The Main Takeaway:

Evaluating the team is a difficult but necessary task. The team should be focused on the project—not their own interpersonal dramas. Ideally, its members should each perform separate functions but also be able to step in for and support one another.

Familial or personal ties between the members is a disadvantage because in place of purely business considerations, unpredictable emotional factors can wreak havoc on the project.

6

NOAH'S SECOND COMING

THE COLD REALITY OF SUNK COSTS

P *remise:*
You decide to go to Israel to visit Jerusalem for a couple of days. You purchase the in-country train tickets and a five-star hotel reservation in advance. Suddenly, only an hour before departure, you

learn that the waters are rising and Jerusalem could soon be hit with one of the worst floods in its long, dry history (not counting the Great Flood, of course). And it's too late to get a refund.

Question:

What should you do? Will you go to Jerusalem anyway to avoid incurring a total loss? After all, weather forecasters are always overly dramatic.

Answer:

Of course not!

That's how it is with investments. The most obvious thing to do is admit that these are sunk costs, lost in the flood. Forget about that money—just enjoy life here, safe and sound and with dry feet. Bad stuff happens, that's a guarantee. Even if we lose things from time to time, will it lower our standard of living? You would risk much more if you went to Jerusalem: how much time and money would you spend trying to escape from a flooded city, not to mention risking your health and even your life?

But in business, people often fail to include sunk costs in their calculations. This is because people are at the heart of every business transaction, and human psychology is such that we gamble with the expectation of winning. Even if we've lost our shirt, we'll stay at the casino with the hope of winning everything back. I do this myself sometimes and will occasionally go to a "flooded Jerusalem." This is one of the key mistakes made by both investors and entrepreneurs.

For instance, we invested a great deal of money, doggedly, and over a long period in a particular company. The team was developing a technology that nobody understood but that everyone expected would be a breakthrough. We poured a ton of resources into it—the founders were great and intensely passionate about the project. Everything seemed to be progressing, but then it just stopped and nothing was working. We invested more money, but to no effect. We replaced the team and added more money. Everyone was optimistic now. But it again ground to a halt. And this kept happening. Eventually, it came down to the simple human desire to recover our losses: after all, we had put so much money, time and effort into this project. The idea was great and the founders were practically like family by then. So we decided to give it one last try.

Then a question arose: What was the value of this wonderful company that, try as we might, we couldn't make work? Maybe someone would pay us $1 million to "buy it for parts," but we had already put $10 million into the thing. That was frustrating. But then we thought: "If we've put so much into it already, why not throw in some more?" And the result was a bottomless pit.

Rule:

Unfortunately, the harsh truth is that the price of a company is what someone will *pay* for it—not what someone has *invested* in it. Even if we had invested $10 million over five years, if a buyer would only give us $1 million tops for it, then the value of this not-quite-operational company was $1 million. The value of a company is determined by how much someone will pay for it now and what its prospects are for growth. If you continue to invest only because you would regret stopping, every successive round of funding will be more painful than the last.

Exception:

Of 100 mice placed in a bucket of milk, 99 will flounder and drown. But one, the most persistent, will paddle at the milk so furiously that they turn it into butter. I have had such cases where a project just wasn't working and everyone had given up on it, but the founders redoubled their efforts, fought and struggled, and got the thing going again with the very last ounce of their strength. Just when it looked as though the project would breathe its last breath, it came to life and began growing. Willpower and determination alone had turned certain defeat into victory.

Does this mean that if you beat your head against the wall long enough, you will eventually break open a hole through which you can climb to a brighter future? In the vast majority of cases, no. I have seen examples of incredible persistence, though. In one, the founder had four children. He had risked everything and suffered a decline in his standard of living, but he believed in his business so much that he was prepared to struggle with it to the end. I had already given up on it when he wrote saying that he had made some progress. Should I believe it? I had faith in the man and the project separately, but not in the two of them together. But I still gave him a little more money. What was motivating me, if not that same damned feeling of infatuation with a project?

Where does such sentimentality come from? The fact is that this particular project was first presented to me at the idea stage, with little more than that sketch on a table napkin mentioned earlier. The project was too risky for our investment fund, but I liked the team and so I initially invested my own funds. The investment fund came on board later. And when the project came to a standstill and began stagnating, my faith in it had not yet dried up, so I stopped risking any more of the shareholders' money and continued to invest my personal funds. And I lost that money. What was my mistake? I should have based my assessment not only on the team but also on the business itself.

Always remember that you should have not only a bright and talented team but also a business, a product, a market of known dimensions, a plan for entering that market, an expected level of demand and the basic math—in short, a lot of boring but very necessary things. When you see the market has a need, the proper distribution channels exist, and that the project could go viral and scale up nicely, only then do you enter the fray.

But what kind of life is it if you never fall in love?

The Main Takeaway:

A wife leaves her husband not because he lost money gambling once but because he kept gambling in the hope of breaking even—only deepening his losses. In other words, if a project has become a financial drain, find a better use for your money. The truism: "Don't throw good money after bad" is true for a reason. Don't throw more money on top of money already lost.

By prolonging the convulsions of a sinking project, you only increase your losses.

Exception:

Let's say that a project is barely moving forward but a proposal is made to make a decisive pivot by changing the start-up's business model, product or scope—in short, by adopting a new strategy. This would warrant additional financing—if, of course, the project has a strong team capable of managing everything.

Rule for the Exception:

Evaluate the new strategy just as carefully as you would a new project.

7

ON REDEMPTIVE MULTIPLICITY

BUSINESS MODELS, BUSINESS PORTFOLIOS AND THE ONE-LEGGED RABBI

P *remise:*
    *Mr. Rabinowitz was a good shoemaker. He worked all day, and although he didn't earn much, he had enough to live on. Then one day, a rich one-legged rabbi came to town who had trouble finding shoes because of his long, six-toed foot. "This rabbi is rich,"
Rabinowitz thought, "and he has an unusual foot that nothing fits. I'll make a special shoe block, sew boots for his foot and charge a fortune for them. Then I won't have to work for peanuts anymore."*

He stopped making ordinary boots and for two weeks, he did nothing but craft the perfect shoe for the rabbi. He used the best leather he could find and even cast a shoe buckle of solid gold.

Question:

Did Mr. Rabinowitz come up with a good idea? Will his business thrive?

Answer:

There are three major problems with one-legged rabbis: there aren't many of them, they can die from various causes and, even more frequently, they move away. It's not much of a business model.

For me, it is important to understand who and where our clients are, how to reach them, and that they are *numerous* and not overly fragmented. When the entire clientele consists of only a couple of one-legged rabbis, if one or more of them unexpectedly dies or moves away, your business will be left without a leg to stand on.

I also want to say that doing business is not easy. I have no desire to criticize anyone for how they launch a business. Everything I say about how to build business models applies primarily to my own line of work. My hope is that my thoughts will be useful in some way to you.

In effect, all business models are good when you have a clear idea of what to do and how to do it. When the numbers are in order, everything else is just a matter of personal choice. I usually choose either of two business models: direct sale of the product to the end user or subscription sales. My least preferred model is selling to major companies or enterprises. I find that sort of transaction unwieldy and unpredictable. And even if you manage to cope with all the difficulties involved, the big players can toss you clear out of the game without warning, leaving you to nurse your hurt feelings—and your losses—alone.

When selling to corporations, the service component far outweighs the product component. The corporate customer tends to demand the same thing, but, as the old business adage goes, "with buttons of pearl and gold trim." Tempted by the prospect of a large order, founders might find themselves devoting enormous resources to modifying the product and maintaining supply. At that point, any thought of creating and promoting a universal, scalable product is lost.

I'd argue to not let the "buttons and trim" override the product development strategy and to instead make luxury features optional through upgrades or subscriptions. Even worse than selling to corporations is selling to small and medium-sized businesses (SMEs). Although there are fewer procedural hurdles involved, each business differs and requires an individualized approach, making a standard solution impossible.

The problem with SMEs that no one can really solve is that their requirements and the cost of finding a paying client can be quite high, even while their willingness to pay and "life-times" are lower. The result is that unit economics goes down the drain. Unit economics are how much a project spends to earn a dollar. If a company is spending 10 dollars to earn one dollar, the unit economics are in the toilet.

As the classic proverb states, "Men of medium height look just like smaller men, but eat like larger men."

Of course, this does not mean that such sales models are bad and should be avoided at all costs. If you know how to sell to major enterprises and SMEs, go right ahead. It's just that I specialize in other models. Actually, I do have experience working with large companies from when we invested in applications for banks and insurance companies. We made numerous mistakes, but through some miracle, we ended up selling to the intended enterprise. However, the very fact that it

took a miracle to succeed convinced me that I didn't want to
venture into that type of morass ever again.

Rule:

For a business, the fewer the customers, the greater the risk.
A company with numerous smaller clients has a better outlook.
Even in nature, multiplicity is more advantageous. If you base
your business on a single large buyer, your fortunes are tied
inextricably to theirs.

My comfort zone is in financial tech, where we deal with
transactions between individual clients and do not cater to a
single Goliath. We deal with a live, developing market, but most
importantly, we can make changes to it. Just compare some
unwieldy banking giant and an ever-changing, nimble user
segment and imagine which you'd rather play with—a huge,
lumbering elephant or a flock of adorable dolphins. I'm for the
dolphins.

There is another consideration you should always keep in
mind. The more customers you have, the greater the chances
that if you develop something really great, someone will come
along and buy you out. There's nothing wrong with this: I
invest in businesses with the express goal of selling them later.
But if we invest in a project that has only three potential buyers
on the market, this greatly reduces the probability of success.

There is another risk here. Let's say we end up in a market
with three major buyers. And let's say four other companies
have developed products very similar to ours and all five of us
are vying for the same buyers. Even if our product is the best,
where is the guarantee that a buyer will snatch it up and pass
over the others? I lived through this exact scenario. A project of

ours outshone the others in every way, and yet the buyer purchased one of our weaker competitors.

Rule (Sad as It Is):
Often buyers don't purchase the best project, but the one managed by the craftiest (and sometimes most underhanded) team.

Question from a Major Product Manufacturer:
Do you base your reluctance to work with major corporations on some subjective value system?

I base this reluctance on personal experience. I've done a lot of work with large corporations and jumped through their many hoops in selling to them. I love stability. Even the process of selling to major corporations can be stable and reliable if, for example, your project has become so large that 500 major companies buy your product in commensurate proportions. However, when you have just one customer who buys the bulk of your products, you run a major risk.

I can understand why some people like selling to large corporations, but this has very little to do with startups. Since this book focuses on bold and crazy ideas, it's probably best to finish discussing corporations. I worked for many years with system integrators, for example, and I know that although this business is very profitable, it receives much less capitalization. This is due not so much to the nature of the market but to the fact that the business is essentially a service and requires large amounts of labor and other costs unique to each client. This lowers the share price/earnings (P/E) ratios.

Maybe I am just a little jaded from dealing with corporations, but I do think that avoiding them is a more practical and wiser approach.

Rule:

All successful projects have something in common: they are universal enough to attract a large number of users who pay for the product or service regularly, over a period of months or years.

Finally, it is worth noting that multiplicity is not necessarily the best possible option under all circumstances. For example, an entrepreneur cannot run 10 businesses at once; he must be as focused as possible and only then will he succeed. Note, however, that this applies only to the entrepreneur: the exact opposite applies to the investor. If the investor puts his whole heart and soul into a single startup and refuses to work with any others until he makes a successful exit from the first, his risk rises exponentially.

Any number of unpredictable situations might arise. For example, you have a good potential market, no storm clouds are gathering on the horizon, you are working out the final details and preparing to release the product for sale when a new technology suddenly appears that makes everything you've done obsolete. This happens all the time. Consider the smartphone market. First, a frenzy of push-button models were all competing for market share when a killer appeared on the scene—the iPhone—and suddenly, all the other players looked dull and uninteresting by comparison.

That's why I recommend that investors diversify their investments by creating a portfolio of startups. For peace of mind and a greater chance of success, it is better to have more projects, rather than fewer, because even the most promising project might fail for some reason, while the rest will serve to soften the financial blow.

Rule:

An investor does not influence an industry: he only keeps his finger on its pulse and monitors threats without exercising any direct leverage over it. Therefore, it is necessary to have a diversified portfolio.

Opinions differ: some say you should have at least 10 projects in your portfolio, and some investment funds do just that. Our funds have more than 100 projects and some people think this is a lot. However, Dave McClure, the founder of 500 Startups, believed that having several thousand projects would increase his chances dramatically. Today, they have thousands of projects and dozens of unicorns.

We have only a few unicorns, but I hope that will change. We lie somewhere between the two extremes of making only rare, pinpoint investments and throwing resources at absolutely everything that moves. We try to find promising projects while they are still at an early stage and then go through the subsequent phases with them, come to better understand the project and the team and, if possible, invest more in them as we go. This strategy provides us with an attractive investment income. At the start, it is very difficult to know which of the projects will become a real star.

To choose between the two extremes, I lean more toward Dave McClure's approach than the idea that you should have only three projects, and that each should become a superstar. The latter approach will cause you much more anxiety and sleepless nights, and the financial return will be lower. If you prefer having fewer irons in the fire, then it's better to become an entrepreneur and focus on a single project. That should make you happy—unless, of course, it doesn't.

The Main Takeaway:

An entrepreneur should focus on one thing only. An investor should focus on identifying his investment strategy and following it.

8

HOW MANY COMPETITORS DO YOU NEED TO BE HAPPY?

WHY IT'S IMPORTANT TO CHERISH YOUR RIVALS

P *remise:*
    You run a venture capital fund. A charming founder comes to you and makes a strong presentation about his project with an excellent speech and outstanding slides. The slide detailing market competition reads, "There are no competitors." Wow! What a rare and wonderful situation! You feel you should definitely invest in the project!

    Question:
    Does anything seem strange to you?

Answer:

Of course it does! This charming founder should be thrown out of the room until he figures out why he has no competitors.

Many founders of lackluster, useless projects happily report during their presentations that they have no competitors and that this gives them a unique advantage. All of my experience has shown me that there can be only two reasons a project has no competitors—either the founder did a poor job of searching for them or else his project is so bad that nobody would want it, much less want to compete with it. It's like the old joke:

Two cowboys are riding on the prairie. Suddenly, a third person rides by so fast that their hats are almost blown off. A few minutes later, he whips by again in the opposite direction. One cowboy asks the other, "Who is that racing around?"

"That's Hard-to-Catch Joe," the second cowboy says.

"Really? Why 'Hard-to-Catch?'"

"Because no one really wants him in the first place."

Rule:

You will definitely have competition. Always.

Even some very good startups suffer from "there's no one else like us in the world" syndrome. I blame it on laziness and infatuation with their own product.

Some inexperienced entrepreneurs simply do not understand what competition is or how to classify it. They see it like this: if I sell iPhones in black cases with stars on them, and you sell iPhones in black cases *without* stars, then we are not competitors. In fact, a competitor is anyone who convinces your potential clients to devote their money and time to them, and not to you. For example, television is a competitor of newspapers.

Competition will always exist because money and time will always be finite. Many people don't like the idea itself and refuse to think about the fact that there are other businesses like theirs on the market. I can sympathize because it is a scary thought. I committed the same mistake as an entrepreneur, thinking that if I just made everything really great, there would be no need to think about the competition.

When we think about competition, we immediately imagine a very fierce but healthy rivalry such as runners with perfect bodies who are poised at the starting block. The gun sounds and they take off in a fair struggle to determine who is the fastest, who is second fastest and who did not prepare properly for the race. It works a little differently in the entrepreneurial world however, because competition is much less straightforward and predictable. In business, the human factor and problems with perception often cause people to underestimate or overestimate their competitors.

I had one such experience. We developed a very good product that we would logically have sold to a large company, despite my wariness about selling to corporations. When I studied the competition, I found several similar products on the market and discovered that, whereas we had been planning to sell our solution for $50,000, our competitors were asking $10 million or more for theirs. We considered this, jazzed ours up a bit more and began asking $1 million for it. All of the companies we showed our product to thought it was great. So, I couldn't understand why, if ours was so cool and everyone was licking their lips when they saw it, they were buying from our competitors for $10 million and not from us.

The reason was that we were an unknown startup with three employees in the US and 50 overseas and no proven track record. We were trying to sell to three large US corporations, all of whom were transparent and public in their dealing. Sitting across from us at the negotiating table were the three managers of these major companies, each of whom had to answer for whatever decision they made. No matter how hard we tried, they didn't buy from us for $1 million, but from our competitors for $10 million because they were a large, publicly traded company that nobody thought would go under next month. And, although there was no way to be certain those companies wouldn't fail, if they did, at least the manager would have had to find some way to justify his decision. He could say that he bought from a reputable company from which everyone buys —how else should he have acted? But if he had purchased from us for $1 million and our company had collapsed the next day, he would have been accused of overlooking the risk of an unstable supplier. As a result, although our product was superior in every way and even though journalists loved it and analysts called it a real breakthrough, sales never took off.

Caveat:

Entrenched corporate habits are beginning to change, such that some major companies now welcome venture capital risk. They understand that smaller, more flexible startup teams are the ones that most often produce innovative and effective solutions, and that to ignore this fact means losing in the larger-scale competition.

Rule:

Know your competition. Consider all of the factors involved, including the most unexpected and unpleasant, keeping in mind that not everything is as straightforward as it might appear. If a startup has no competitors, stop and study it more closely until you figure out what is wrong.

After you have identified your competition, a fundamentally important stage begins that directly affects the fate of your startup: the search for competitive advantages and competitive positioning. If I see that an entrepreneur does not understand his competitive advantages, I will not invest in his project. He must have a clear understanding of what makes his project better than that of his competitors and of how to bring those advantages to market. In fact, the ability to position oneself on the market is no less important than having competitive advantages in the first place.

It is very fashionable for startups to draw a quadrant and place their project in the upper-right corner or to draw a table comparing the advantages of their project versus the competition. Rivals might have anywhere from five to eight strongpoints, while the project under consideration boasts 10—never mind that the two extra points are of little or no value to the client.

Of course, we dismiss such self-assessments. In reality, there are only two types of competitive advantages we look for: if it creates a new product or service and is able to generate demand, or does something familiar, but much more effectively.

Timing is also a critical factor. As a rule, dozens of different teams might be working at the same time to produce the same innovation, and all are responding to the same emerging consumer need. This makes it important to not only be the first to offer your product to the client but also to line up your competitive advantage in advance. This is especially true of technologies based on the latest scientific discoveries and major innovations—often referred to as "deep tech"—with its long development and production cycle. The portfolio of our venture capital funds includes several such complex projects whose fates remain uncertain, and it is too early to say whether they will be huge successes or major losses. This is why we avoid taking on projects with especially long development cycles, such as pharmacology or medical devices.

Sometimes the competition can come from unexpected corners and in surprising forms. The classic example is how NASA invested huge sums to develop a ballpoint pen that could write in zero gravity, while Soviet cosmonauts simply used pencils to accomplish the same task.

The Main Takeaway:

Look very closely at product positioning: it is important to identify your competitors and be certain that there is demand for what you are offering.

No matter what your friends, family members, business coaches or a bunch of British scientists tell you, the consumer is the ultimate arbiter. He or she determines whether your product or service is actually new and effective and worth buying—or that it isn't, and they pass it by with a shrug of their shoulders.

If you don't see a product's competitive advantages, better to pass on it.

9

LEARNING TO COOPERATE VS. GETTING OFFENDED EASILY

ON INVESTORS' HERD INSTINCT AND DIRTY TRICKS

P *remise:*
   Simon and Peter are out picking mushrooms. Simon carries a small basket, but he knows the best places to find mushrooms. Peter has a large basket but doesn't know the first thing about mushrooms. Simon thinks, "If I show Peter where the best mush-

rooms are found, he'll know what I know—and he's got a huge basket!"

Question:

What should Simon do? Should he protect his prized mushroom patches by only showing Peter where the small and flavorless mush- rooms grow or should he show Peter his choice locations?

Answer:

Although experienced mushroom gatherers might disagree with me, I'd tell Simon he should share his prized spots with Peter. After all, Simon himself wouldn't like eating small and flavorless mush- rooms—even if they were sweetened by the knowledge that Peter was choking on them, too!

To continue with the mushroom analogy, the forest can be a mysterious and dangerous place. You might encounter a bear— or worse. But if *two* people meet a bear, at least one of them has a good chance of escaping. What's more, our hypothetical Peter might have interesting and useful knowledge and skills that Ivan could acquire. After all, Peter knew enough to get his hands on a very large basket. And in the end, two heads are always better than one.

What does all this have to do with investment? To an outside observer, venture capitalists might seem like misers sitting on their sacks of gold. True, the occasional investor might fit this mold, but in my experience, most are sociable folk who tend to operate in herds. Knowing the market and its dynamics is our bread and butter, and it is almost impossible to gain this knowledge by distancing yourself completely from the investment environment. That is why we meet often, talk shop, give each other leads on this or that project and generally help each other in whatever way we can. You help me today, and tomorrow I'll return the favor. An investor who remains aloof and disconnected will soon have no idea of what is happening in the market.

If 90 percent of my projects were failures, maybe I would be more sullen and standoffish, but since many of my projects are booming, I'm motivated to get out there and interact with others. It is like chess: if you play inferior opponents, your own game suffers and you go soft. That is why I like meeting with my equals in business: I am happy to share my concerns with them and openly discuss the many issues that arise in our line of work.

Question from a Capitalist Shark:

What about competitors and their habit of sabotaging others, backhanded dealing and elbowing out their rivals? One gets the impression that investors are naïve little angels.

This is the amusing paradox of our industry: sure, we all hang out together, share experiences and generally "play nice," but some very nasty—and, some might say, downright ugly—situations can arise. But if you're an investor, you can't afford to get upset every time someone crosses you. After all, you might wind up working on other projects with that person. You don't have to be best friends, but you do need to put your money in the same pot with them—and money, unlike people, won't let you down. That is why it is better not to get yourself and your fellow investor all riled up—however unpleasant that person might be.

With co-investment, you share the risks. Co-investing also adds confidence early on that you'll be able to "pass through the valley of death" successfully—that is, to get through the period when the project is no longer just a dream anymore, but has yet to conquer the market. When the money has run out, and the next-stage investors are saying, "Come back tomorrow."

Of course, investors tend to rely, at least partially, on the hunches and expertise of their fellow investors—although this confidence is not always justified. Sometimes, an abundance of "star investors" prompts everyone to base their faith on each other's involvement, rather than on the merits of the project itself. The most striking example is the Theranos company, whose valuation rose to $10 billion before it came out that the technology at its core was a sham, causing its stocks to crash and burn overnight. Nobody—not even the "star investors"—had bothered to check this out beforehand.

Rule:

An investor cannot afford to let himself become offended easily. There can be a lot of serious elbowing and jostling on the market, so if you are unable to take it all in stride, better to stay out of the fight: your peace of mind is more important.

Why all of this tough talk, anyway? It's because everything revolves around money. I have often seen one party try to dilute another's share, squeeze someone out of a deal, impose impossible conditions at the last minute or use tricky legal maneuvers against competitors. Naturally, all this is unpleasant and makes me want to say a few choice words to such people. But I have come to realize that doing so is simply unproductive. As common as these ugly situations are, it is best to avoid such people entirely. However, if the person isn't a total bastard but simply has a difficult manner or interests that don't happen to coincide with yours at the moment, you can work through such problems, putting pragmatic concerns above emotions.

The Main Takeaway:

Co-investing is both possible and worthwhile, but you should always make your own judgment call about each project. Of course, other investors are also risking their money, but it is a good idea to ask how they view the project and why they want a partnership.

10

A HEALTHY BOARD OF DIRECTORS

GAUGING A STARTUP'S PROBLEMS BY THE VOLUME OF THE SCREAMS

P *remise:*

A company's board of directors includes a swan, a lobster and a trout. Although they started out with the same vision for the company's development, at some point they all began advocating different approaches. To restore balance, the decision is made to change the membership of the board.

Question:

Which changes should they make? Should they add another trout, swan and lobster, or perhaps give a seat to every form of fauna that has an interest in this company's affairs?

Answer:
It's amazing this business functioned at all, but it now seems to be dead in the water.

I have served, and continue to serve on a great many boards of directors. Some people consider this duty a mere formality while others attribute great importance to it. From my point of view, the board of directors plays a very clear, utilitarian role. A closer look at any board will tell you why a particular business is either failing or booming. This is due less to *which* questions are discussed at meetings than *how* they are discussed.

Let's start with some basics. Not all directors can participate in meetings of the board of directors—in some on which I serve, I am only an observer. Usually, observers are included who hold a significant stake in the business and who have the ability to influence decisions. It is also a way to avoid letting board meetings turn into a meeting of shareholders.

What is the purpose of a board of directors? In principle, it is very possible to do without one when a business is just getting started. Although it is very important for a startup that the investor's representative have a presence, there is no need to formalize this relationship.

However, the board begins to play a major role during the transition to growth and even more in a fully developed company.

In an ideal world, the board of directors should not be very large and should include representatives of the founders and leading investors. Most importantly, however, their consultations should be amicable, productive and focused on solving specific issues without ever ending in deadlock. Squabbles on a board of directors are usually a very alarming sign.

Don't confuse a board of directors with a parliament, much less with a government. A board is essentially an advisory body

—that is, it makes decisions on important issues but does not function on a daily basis. Managers can turn to a board during emergencies, but normally it meets periodically, with members continuing their communication between meetings.

Here's a typical task for a board of directors: a new, very high-powered person joins the team and must be given ample motivation to stay with the project. It would be a shame if he received only the standard pay package, deemed it insufficient and left. The founder does not have the right and, sometimes, enough experience to formulate the best offer, and the decision requires the consent of all interested parties. In such cases, the board of directors convenes and resolves the issue or reaches a decision. Or sometimes the chance for an interesting deal arises, but it requires the permission of the board of directors because the sum in question exceeds what the charter allows. Each company has its own list of questions that only a board of directors' quorum can decide, and the nature of these issues can vary widely from one company to the next.

There is nothing particularly romantic or exciting about the way boards hold their meetings. The work is very straightforward. With successful companies, such meetings are a pleasure: the board members deal with clear and interesting challenges related to growth and scaling. But with companies where growth has stalled, the tone and content of the meetings are notably different. Board members are more likely to discuss how to keep the business afloat than plans for expansion. Of course, this is often unpleasant. On the other hand, it brings a great deal of satisfaction when you help a team turn the situation around and achieve success.

I consider it a sign of trouble when the mood on the board of directors turns sour. It might only result in a few negative episodes without culminating in disaster. Some problems, after all, are inevitable. But if the business is booming, conflicts are usually rare and easily resolved. Otherwise, protracted crises on the board might signal systemic problems that are best identified while the patient can still be saved.

Rule:

When a business is doing well, serving on the board of directors is a pleasure.

Exception:

Even when the business is doing fine, any number of factors can complicate the work of the board of directors. And, because we are all imperfect, the human factor is often to blame.

I once served on the board of directors of a US company. Everything was going well until the chairman unexpectedly put his son on the board as well. Why? That's a good question. The most likely reason is that he wanted to gain greater control over the company and use his son to snoop around for insider information. That by itself was unpleasant, even more because his son was not a good worker and the company was unhappy with him. It ended with the founders deciding to fire this high-ranking offspring. From that moment on, the board meetings turned into a feud. Previously, if the chairman had criticized the team for something, he always did it constructively and helped find solutions to complex problems. But after his son was dismissed, he began taking out his anger on everyone and openly giving hell to management, with or without cause. Fortunately, there were mechanisms in place that made it possible to remove him from the board as well.

Such behavior always surprises me—that is, when people who seem to be adults and who are far from newcomers to business suddenly begin acting like little children. And in such situations, quite apart from any ethical considerations, a very unambiguous legal factor arises as well. Every member of the board of directors is obligated to act in the company's interests. If I work against those interests, I risk not only strong censure from my colleagues but also a serious talking-to from lawyers that might culminate in a court case.

However, "sophisticated" such palace intrigue and infighting might appear from the outside, they are essentially sandbox skirmishes. It might happen that one investor starts playing games by announcing that he won't take part in any board meetings if a certain investor is also present. Although there might be some grounds for such reluctance, we are all adults after all and should be able to get along. Why not meet one-on-one with the person in question and try to work out your differences in a civil way, rather than resorting to under-handed, Machiavellian schemes?

There is nothing inherently wrong or unhealthy about wanting or not wanting to serve on a board of directors. The board only exists to discuss money matters. Its members are not trying to land a Nobel Prize—they are simply trying to manage a business in which they have invested their funds. To do that, they just want to know what is happening with the project. After all, a board member's job is not to strut around in an expensive jacket, puff on a cigar and vote on measures by flipping a coin. He or she must study tons of materials, do their homework, have a full grasp of what's happening on the market and know what the competition is doing. And just to be clear, board members get paid absolutely nothing for all their trouble —which is considerable. My main motivation in serving is to ensure that the company prospers and pays back my initial investment many times over. I am there simply to influence operations and help.

Serving on a board of directors is also a major responsibility. It sometimes makes sense to appoint people to the board who have specific competencies that are of greatest benefit to the company.

Of course, serving on a board of directors is not the only way to play a role in the life of a startup. Acting as a mentor is also common. This is a very specific form of assistance. As a rule, though, I don't take a fee for advice and mentoring, although many others do. Some mentors have a standard practice of demanding both payment and a percentage of the business.

This isn't my favorite approach. Why? Because I feel my advice isn't worth much if I don't have my own money invested in the business.

This reminds me of an old joke about a rabbi and a chicken coop. Some villagers come to their rabbi and complain that the chickens are dying. He tells them, "Draw a circle on the floor of the coop and put all the chickens in it." A short time later, they return and report that more chickens have died. The rabbi says, "Divide the coop into four quadrants and place the chickens in the upper right quadrant." It doesn't help, and the villagers come to the rabbi a third time. Before he can even open his mouth they tell him, "All the chickens are dead." He shakes his head in sorrow. "What a pity," he says, "I still have so many ideas."

That's how I feel about offering outside consultation and mentorship on projects in which I'm not risking anything, but from which I often receive various perks and other benefits on someone else's tab. This brings us back to the key rule of almost any undertaking—that is, *to have more skin in the game*. Still, not all mentors are selfish predators. Some are even extremely helpful.

What do brilliant startups want from a mentor? It might be easier to say what they *don't* want.

To paraphrase an American saying, "Wherever you try to kiss a startup, its ass is everywhere."

A couple of years ago, this happened to me with the founder of an AI startup. Some entrepreneurs, including some successful founders with whom I had worked, introduced me to a project. I liked the idea and knew the team. I spent a lot of time with them, trying to help them hone their vision for the market.

And, of course, I gave them a small check as part of the current round, agreeing that once all the documents were approved, I would give them a larger check.

And then, everything fell apart.

First, the founders grew disappointed in their idea and split up. The one who remained with the project offered me a new vision that I considered flawed. He didn't listen to me, but I turned out to be right. This left the founder resenting me.

After trying several less than ethical iterations of his idea, the founder finally settled on an interesting approach and managed to attract investment. He also decided to "forgive" me.

I chose not to sue over the small check I had given because life has a way of working out such things on its own. But this was a vivid illustration of the proverb mentioned above. It wasn't all that bad, actually. Even one determined one jerk can't discourage a whole team of talented people. In this particular case, he finally understood and bought us out.

So, what is it that startups want from mentors? Each has its own set of challenges. One might want to consult on whether to hold a round of investment, and if so, in what form and when? Should they seek investors from Germany, Israel, the US or multiple countries? Should they hold an intermediate round or aim for a big one straight away? Which set of figures should they post for each type of round? What is the best way to make a pitch? Founders with whom I have already worked sometimes come to me with personal problems, but most often with financial concerns. These tend to be symptomatic of larger problems with the business itself.

Before creating his startup, one fellow had been earning $10,000 per month working for a corporation. Now he only earned $3,000–$5,000 per month. At which point, a familiar refrain began: "Let's raise my salary before my wife kicks me out of the house." This is no joke. I hear this kind of thing several times a month. One person points to the fact that the average salary in their country is much higher. Another says, "But I used to earn more." I answer, "Okay, you used to receive a certain sum every month. Now, you own 33 percent of a growing company that is already valued at $30 million, meaning that your share is worth $10 million. But I agree. Let's give back your share and, instead, pay you the salary you used to earn. Do you agree?" You can guess their answer.

Such shortsighted thinking is worse than stealing, in my opinion. I believe it's okay to pay large salaries to top employees who hold a small stock option in the company. The founder, however, holds the great majority of shares, and they must learn to get by on starvation rations until the company soars into the stratosphere. If you try to live glamorously on investors' money, you are simply pulling out resources that the business needs to thrive. I have seen many promising companies fail because team members reached an impasse over salaries.

Rule:

A project should never turn into a business whose main purpose is not to grow, but to ensure that the founders never suffer from want.

The Main Takeaway:

Share your experience, connections and knowledge with a business in which you have invested, but don't try to take over as operational manager of the project.

11

THE MOST UNPLEASANT CHAPTER

HOW INVESTORS SPEND MOST OF THEIR TIME

P *remise:*
> *You are an international investor—not yet a giant on the global market but not a neophyte either: you are somewhere between an angel and a professional investor who has a portfolio of several dozen early-stage projects.*
> *Question:*
> *How do you spend most of your time?*

Answer:

Working on documents. This is the least attractive aspect of an investor's job.

An outside observer might think that investors have a glamorous life like Jeff Bezos, financing rocket ship projects, trading in a yacht for a super yacht and attending parties with Leonardo DiCaprio and his most recent 24-year-old girlfriend. There is a little bit of truth to this: angel investors do spend a lot of their time at mixers or clubs with other investors where they can meet the right people, listen to pitches and get a sense of which way the economic winds are blowing. There is also an endless stream of phone calls, most of which sound like this: "Hey there, Joe. You know, there's this really cool project and we were just wondering if you'd like to invest in it." However, despite all this wonderful idleness, an investor must stay focused. Like a doctor who is constantly on call, you never know from which direction the next professional challenge will appear, or what form it will take.

As an investor's portfolio expands, his life becomes more complicated. Several times a week, we survey the latest startups to see if anything worthwhile has appeared. And once a week, we review our own portfolio projects and identify problem areas requiring our attention. One project might be due for a new round of investment, another might be experiencing an unexpected problem and a third is growing so fast that we can barely keep up with it. Managing just 10 projects can keep a person up at night. Imagine receiving 300 pages of investment legalese written by overpaid lawyers who specialize in obscuring the facts and their true intentions.

This is when the process of painstakingly threading your way through the Amazonian jungle begins. Just try sitting for five hours and reading every word of a user's agreement on anything from, say, a frying pan to an iPhone. This, of course, is the stage at which mistakes often occur. One person writing the fine print might have made an unintentional blunder, while another has deliberately tried to mislead you. As a result, you can never just click the box "Accept terms" without double-checking everything. Still, some people skim over these details because they are too lazy to do the work. And besides, the founders swore on their mothers' graves that everything was on the up and up—and how can you not trust them? But once these things slip past uncorrected or unresolved, they almost inevitably lead to problems—some are small and some are major tragedies.

This is why, when an angel investor morphs into an "archangel," they bring in rather extensive legal support—and the stronger it is, the less likely someone will manage to throw a monkey wrench in the works. In the absence of competent specialists, all you can do is pray. In fact, professionals have an expression for it: *to pay and pray.* After that, the choice is yours. You can either throw your money in every direction in the hope that the people you're paying will behave honorably, or you can spend a huge amount of time consulting with lawyers and reading everything yourself. And no magical, cookie cutter-type form exists that you can use for every project. Each agreement for a new round of investment is developed from scratch. It is based on an analysis of the project's prospects and lays out specific points relevant to that particular undertaking. After that, we start working with lawyers from the opposite angle because founders are generally willing to spend much more on legally registering transactions than angel investors are. This is, in part, because founders make use of investors' funds for such needs, and not their own. And, for the biggest projects, lawyers often take payment in stock options.

Lawyers love startups because both sides spend loads of money on laying out the ground rules. A veritable street match begins to determine which side is the coolest. What's more, lawyers are often more intent on stirring up trouble between business partners than bringing them into agreement. In this respect, lawyers resemble quarrelsome street kids who simply make it impossible to conduct negotiations, with their habit of telling everyone what to do and their love of doublespeak and deadlocks. It reminds me of a joke about a doctor and his son. "Dad!" the son of a doctor exclaims, "I've cured Madame Rabinovich! You've been treating her for years and couldn't cure her. But one attempt by me, and she's all better!" "Oy vey, David!" the father says, shaking his head. "What have you done? It was her money that put you through medical school and internships at the best clinics in Germany and Israel—and all because I kept bringing her in for treatment. But now, you putz, you've gone and cured her!"

The Main Takeaway:

If you are certain you won't lose your faith in humanity even if you are regularly cheated out of millions of dollars, then go right ahead and sign documents without reading them. Otherwise, hire an honest lawyer and learn to speed-read.

A lot of time is spent not only on routine legal matters, but also on financial affairs. You must decide at what time and at which price you should issue options for employees and how best to draw up and execute a budget. A startup should always be able to turn a profit, or at least stay afloat until the next round of investment while maintaining positive unit economics.

Finally, for any transaction—unless it is occurring at an unusually early stage or conducted by an ultra-reliable business partner—you should conduct due diligence to verify the project's legal and financial condition. Otherwise, you might discover one day that you have numerous debts, lawsuits or problems with intellectual property rights.

12

COMING IN FROM THE COLD (A TRANSITIONAL CHAPTER OF EQUAL IMPORTANCE FOR BOTH INVESTORS AND STARTUPS)

A FEW TIPS ON SQUEEZING A CAMEL THROUGH THE EYE OF A NEEDLE

P *remise:*
    You've come up with an innovative startup for effortlessly passing camels through the eyes of needles. Of course, you've thought everything over, crunched the numbers and have come to the easiest part—finding an investor. It's a sure thing. You compile a database with the names and addresses of 100 business angels and investment funds and write a polite letter pitching your project. "Well, dear friend," it reads, "I've created a startup that will make us billionaires. Just give me the word, and I will send you the details. Sincerely—."

Question:

Should you take a deep breath and send out your letter, anticipating a miracle?

Answer:

No. Exhale slowly while stepping away from the computer. Do not press "Send."

Most investors' lives are a constant struggle with a torrent of incoming proposals from founders, who, with varying degrees of perseverance, are trying to convince them to invest money in their projects. Just multiply the number of projects in our portfolio by 3,000 and you'll have an idea of how many proposals we receive each year.

But even that number is just the tip of the iceberg. Many more founders try to catch our eye, but only the best manage to do so. We'll talk more about that later.

Let's start with the projects at the top. Here we find the whole swirling vortex of brilliant ideas and sure-fire startups. They come into our field of vision in different ways, including through personal contacts of mine or one of our team members. We also receive proposals through email, texting service and every other Internet-based form of communication ever invented.

We quickly cull out 90 percent of these projects because the people submitting them were too lazy to do the basic homework. Here's a few examples of failed attempts to impress an investor—in this case, yours truly.

1. I received an email copied to literally 200 other recipients—no kidding! It reads something like this: "Each of you should give whatever you can because we really need the money." Of course, I don't even read such letters. Keep in mind that all negotiations

on projects and financing are a deeply intimate and personal thing, and everything is decided on an individual basis. Mass mailing such requests is borderline offensive.

2. Another classic example: "I would like to offer you a project—the latest thing in the catering market." The sender addressed me by name and had apparently heard something about me, but hadn't bothered to learn that I have no involvement in the food preparation business. I truly wonder what prompted this person to write to me specifically. Carefully study the specialization of the investor you are contacting and never assume that pineapples grow on pine trees.

3. The following query letter consisted of only a few sentences, but they were enough to kill my interest in the project. "Greetings Mr. Ryabenkiy. Are you still in the investing game? I have an IT project. Would you like to know the details?" This sounds almost like the joke, "Joe, is it true that you've stopped drinking cognac in the morning?" Instead of asking pointless questions (of course I'm in the investing business—I'm not a deep sea fisherman or mushroom picker), the sender should tell me about themself and their project as clearly and concisely as possible. After all, they probably won't get a second chance.

4. A separate category belongs to bizarre metaphysical proposals to create this or that "true religion" or to unify and save humanity. Honestly, though, I don't like to even discuss such things.

Rule:

If you are not personally acquainted with the investor, you will probably have only one chance to submit a letter and present yourself and your project as well as you can. Keep in mind, also, that you might end up in a one-on-one interview with the very real person who will read your letter, so you should express at least a modicum of respect. Think about how you are writing, to whom and why, and your chances for securing investment will increase significantly. Otherwise, your letter might wind up in the box marked "Museum of Strange Query Letters."

I must qualify this by explaining that combing through piles of proposals is only part of our practice, and if we had not gone out looking for promising founders on our own, we would never have become successful investors. This is because significantly fewer startups have made their way to us with a blind pitch than those we found ourselves. Referrals also play an important role in our business. These include referrals from our business partners, other investment funds, entrepreneurs with whom we already work and business accelerators. These are "warmer" calls although, even here, a lot depends on how much we trust the source.

But you should never underestimate those determined entrepreneurs who break through all the barriers to reach our desk without any personal connections whatsoever. I often hear reproaches directed at investors who refuse to consider all cold callers, who lock themselves in their own hermetic little world and dive into a pool of gold coins like Scrooge McDuck. This is a mistake, of course. I just looked and found that we have more than a dozen projects in our portfolio that came in from the cold. And they're not just gathering dust either: we have already made successful exits from two of them. This is an excellent result, and it proves that anything is possible if you want it badly enough and can convince others that you're capable.

Question from a Tormented Entrepreneur:

Does this mean that if you make a halfway decent impression, you can count on at least meeting with a potential investor over a cup of coffee?

I wouldn't want to get anyone's hopes up because the likelihood of this happening is low. Most investment funds have a strict hierarchy: first, a junior analyst reviews your project, and so on up the ladder to the chief specialist. Although some investors are open to personal communication, I can't say I'm one of them. There simply aren't enough hours in the day to meet with everyone. But if something really intrigues me, I'll try to respond to the inquiry and make contact. This shortens the usual distance between investor and founder.

I want to end this chapter on an optimistic or encouraging note, but the truth is that investors must process an enormous amount of information in a very short time. Once, my analysts had accumulated an enormous backlog of projects. I got a little impatient with them and decided to help—or rather, show them the correct way to analyze proposals. It took me only 15 minutes to sort through approximately 200 projects. In some cases, I didn't even have to read anything: a glance at how the text was laid out on the page indicated that some projects were definitely no good, whereas others warranted further consideration. I wound up selecting three projects that were more or less worthy and told my analysts, "Give these a closer look, but toss out everything else."

This raises a question: how many babies have I thrown out with the bathwater? It's hard to say. I've definitely thrown out some. Take inDriver, for example. This is a trip aggregator that differs from services like Uber in that the client, and not the system, sets the price. I didn't see any promise in it. I knew of similar projects but nothing had ever come of them. In the end, a friend of mine not only became interested in the project but even went to the trouble of flying to meet with the team. After that, the project really took off. It's now going gangbusters and has expanded to locations all around the world.

An even funnier thing happened concerning Victor Shaburov. Victor is the Director of Cameos for Snapchat, the company that bought his earlier project, Looksery, for $150 million. We once had lunch and took a selfie together. Victor offered to send me the photo through Snapchat, but I had never used or installed the app because I am definitely not part of their target audience. We decided to correspond through Facebook, and when I found him there, I discovered that Victor had written to me two years before with an offer to invest in Looksery. I never even opened that message because I would never think to check Facebook messenger for a pitch. Now, he goes around telling everyone that I missed out on a $150 million deal. He might be right.

The Main Takeaway for Investors:

Limit who can contact you directly by establishing a set of qualifying criteria. Otherwise, you'll have no time for anything else. At the same time, don't shut yourself off in an analytical bubble or you'll lose your instincts for spotting a winner.

The Main Takeaway for Entrepreneurs:

"Ask, and it shall be given you; seek, and ye shall find; knock, and it shall be opened unto you: For every one that asketh receiveth; and he that seeketh findeth; and to him that knocketh it shall be opened." —Matthew 7:7-8

PART II

CANON FOR STARTUPS

1

WHERE TO GET THE MONEY

A STARTUP'S PATH OF FINANCIAL REBIRTH

P *remise:*
You've come up with a good business idea and thought everything through properly. Now you need to find money somewhere. You have several options: borrow it from your distant uncle whom you don't get along with; take a bank loan using the old house you inherited as collateral; ask your local mobster who always has

ready cash and who is always ready to break the bones of anyone who doesn't pay him back; or write to the director of a major investment fund.

Question:

Whom should we ask for money?

Answer:

Everyone gets their money from wherever they can. It's not for me to judge. But the safest option is to borrow it from your uncle— and you never know: you might even wend up on speaking terms again.

On the one hand, the task of attracting money is purely situational and extremely personal. And on the other hand, some standard and fairly straightforward patterns exist. Let's look at them.

You can draw different conclusions about the strange times we're living in, but one thing has definitely improved: the time from the birth of an idea to its implementation has been reduced to a minimum. As recently as 30 years ago, a startup required hundreds of thousands, if not millions of dollars to get off the ground. Today, the initial steps usually cost between $10,000 and $20,000. But the eternal question remains: where to find that money? My advice is to start with yourself. If you are convinced that this project is for you and that you're ready to change the world, put up the initial capital yourself.

After you have accomplished something on that basis, approach your family and friends. In fact, that's why this is called the *friends and family* stage of financing. I am convinced that this is how it should be done. If you aren't confident enough in your project to put your own money down, and if your friends and relatives don't have enough faith in it to lend their support, why would a stranger want to invest in it—especially when that person will, by necessity, be far more demanding and critical of the project? This also serves as an excellent filtering mechanism and safety valve that saves you from taking on mountains of bank debt or taking a hit from a mobster's brass knuckles—or the other hard knocks this world has to offer.

If you are a first-time entrepreneur with no track record and you write to investors saying, "Give me money and I'll turn the world on its head," it is very unlikely anyone will pull out their checkbook. They would be right to be skeptical. But if you had risked your own money and your friends and relatives had lined up behind you, it would already give you a certain favorable reputation. It would indicate that you believe in what you are doing and you have convinced others to believe too. But if you and those closest to you were unwilling to take a risk on the project, you won't have much of a lever with which to turn the world upside down.

At the next stage, you might turn to business incubators/accelerators, or angel investors who might also take an interest in your project. We've already looked at angel investors, but what are business incubators/accelerators? They serve as a growth vitamin of sorts. For projects that already have a clear vision and understanding of where they're going, an accelerator can help them get there faster. Business accelerators have clearly defined and proven methods and connections. Unfortunately, really good business accelerators are rare because there are too many charlatans out there who are ready to take your money in return for nothing more than fluff and fanfare. High-quality business accelerators don't make empty promises, and they don't accept all comers either. If you decide to go this route, look carefully at who has already worked with the accelerator in question and what they say about it.

Your next stop: professional players in the form of either investment funds or archangels. These focus exclusively on investing, and they are not amateurs. Whereas founders often finance projects out of pocket in the early stages, professional players can provide much larger sums raised from investors, to whom they must answer. This is part of the normal life cycle of a successful investor: at some point, they are likely to find themselves in charge of other people's financial flows. When professionals come on board, the whole approach to the business changes. Professionals have their own metrics for determining success and they help because they know every step of the process and have the experience of working with other projects that have succeeded. They can share this experience, as well as their connections—both horizontal and vertical.

Strategic investors require a special mention here. On the one hand, it is always interesting to work with a strategic investor, but on the other, their participation calls for caution. A strategic investor differs from an ordinary investor in that they will not just give you money, but might also be your client and be able to guide you in a particular market. This can be very useful for many technology-based projects. The downside is that once you have a strategic investor, all other investors will lose interest in you. They understand that the strategic investor has effectively limited your market share, and that as a result, all other investors will gain nothing from working with you.

Banks are another potential source of funding, but startups should use them only during the growth stage. This enables the business to avoid cash shortfalls and to develop without interruption. Although paying off this type of loan is a special form of torture, a fast-growing project can use such funds to address a short-term cash crunch and avoid diluting its ownership share.

Conclusion: if your project is strong, the money will come looking for you. But even then, effort is required. It is important to understand which source, entity and form of financing is best for you at each stage of the project.

The Main Takeaway:

When contacting an investor, be concise and specific. Perfect your "elevator pitch": it will open doors for you. And, of course, be clear on who you are contacting and for what you are asking.

2

THE WORLD'S SHORTEST GUIDE TO STAGES AND ROUNDS

FROM A TO AAAAAAA

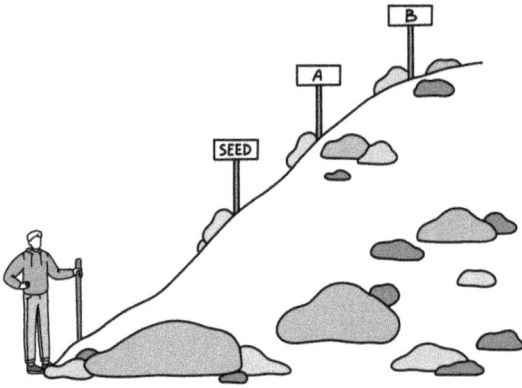

P *remise:*
       At a trendy hipster café, you overhear an interesting conversation between two bearded men discussing the "seed stage" and how they will both become unicorns soon.

Question:
       Who are these people—startup founders or farmers growing magic mushrooms on the edge of a mysterious forest?

Answer:

In all likelihood, these are startup founders—in the flesh! This could be you, my dear reader. However, the fact that the project these men are discussing is at the "seed stage" does not even remotely guarantee that it will become a unicorn—or any other mythological creature, for that matter.

Let's take a closer look. At the "friends and family" stage of financing, you assemble your team and convince yourself and your loved ones that you are doing something important, and not just hanging around and drinking beer with your buddies. You are perfecting your pitch and identifying your strengths.

Next comes the so-called "pre-seed" stage. At this point, you have a prototype of your product, some beta users and a need for money to finalize the technologies involved. You make your first attempts to sell the product to users, analyze your mistakes, hammer out the bugs, undergo market validation and, with a clear head and a clean conscience, set out to find an investor.

This is usually when angel investors appear, and based on the results of your activities, you can apply to business accelerators and incubators.

Now the product is ready and you have to promote it. You are not yet moving to full-scale development, but making a trial run with a single market and one type of customer. This is called the seed stage. This is when angels, archangels and seed funds can join the project. You receive much larger infusions of funding and make much more ambitious plans. Whereas it was not so important where you got your funding in the initial stage (as long as you didn't give anyone a majority share in the company), in the seed stage, the sources of funding take on major importance. Why? Because both the money and the context in which it is given matter. It is very important which ecosystem of future financing you find yourself in. If you start working with business partners who are already integrated into a particular market, then you can use them as stepping stones to make it easier to go through the subsequent stages of development.

It is important to choose the right investors at the seed stage. If they share your vision, they will give you bridge loans at critical junctures and introduce you to and help you with investors at the next stage.

The seed stage is followed by "Stage A." Some people use letters to label the stages, although it would be more accurate to use a combination of numbers, letters and signs. Some refer to stages A, B, C and others use A1, B1, A2 and so on, depending on the imagination of the investors, companies and lawyers involved. Stage A is measured in millions and tens of millions of dollars. Later stages can be measured in hundreds of millions, and sometimes billions, of dollars although this is more common prior to an IPO.

Stage A involves fairly weighty investment funds with impressive financial clout. All subsequent stages differ only in the size of the investment check. Taken together, they are often called the "growth stage." This stage arrives when the technology is fully functional, the path forward is clearly marked, your client base is well defined and the ultimate success of the project depends only on the quantity and quality of the gas you put in the tank.

Between the seed and growth stages, your project must run a harrowing gauntlet. This is often called "the valley of death" because the whole thing can go into a stall from which it might never recover. You have already raised the seed money—which wasn't particularly difficult. But at this point, what have you actually sold to the world? Only a dream! This is when a strange psychological paradox occurs. When someone only promises to do something and places a high price tag on it, he is essentially selling a dream or a vision of what should later become a reality. And it just so happens that investors and business angels have a weakness for such visions and are eager to shower them with money. And that's when the harsh reality of everyday life hits. The project is growing and needs to enter the next stage, but now you are not selling a dream, but the hard reality of a product or service. Your job now is not to win over romantic investors but to convince pragmatic ones interested only in the bottom line. "Let's take a closer look at your growth," they say. "You say you're going to sell in this market to these clients, but how much does it cost you to attract each one? You have brought in approximately 100 potential buyers, but how long did it take you to get them and how likely are you to multiply their number?"

This is when the math can strangle a project to death. It's when investors take a good hard look at the indicators and the unit economics that many startups begin to buckle. The project needs to start turning a profit, but the team is still finalizing the product. The team doesn't fully understand who their clients are yet. Sometimes, it also happens that startups with huge turnovers in the millions cannot advance any further simply because their basic finances begin to float. When this happens, the business has entered the valley of death.

I recently witnessed a typical example of a startup failing to navigate the valley of death. We bought into the "dream" of a startup and the product found customers. I loved the project and didn't want to let go, but all the figures indicated that we should have bailed yesterday—if not last month. The startup had already had a lot of experience on the education market and the vision was inspiring, but during its implementation, the team took a small wrong turn. As a result, they spent $1,000 for every new customer but earned only $100 per month from them. The unit economics were in bad shape. And the longer the company continued like this, the more it cost to bring in new clients. Worse, because it required trained employees to personally enlist each new client, it was necessary to scale up the sales staff to expand the client base. That shot the price up from $1,000 to $5,000 for each new client. At that point, the business could never hope to generate a positive income.

The Main Takeaway:

To make it through the valley of death, you need to prepare in advance. Although optimists rule the world, optimism does not exclude realism. Calculation errors and overly optimistic assumptions can be costly.

3

THE PRICE OF AN IDEA

THE PROBLEM WITH THE SACRED COW

P*remise:*
    You've come up with a brilliant idea for a startup. Although it's only on paper at the moment, your calculations are elegant, your formulas are spot on and your flow charts are impressive. Everything looks great and will definitely work. You have no

money of your own to make it happen, so you consider approaching an investor.

Question:

Will you submit a detailed plan of the project or omit key elements, at least for now, so that no one steals this brilliant idea?

Answer:

Don't waste your time submitting anything.

Since the beginning of time, people have fantasized about how nice it would be to fly through the sky like a bird or swim the seas like a fish. These were wonderful and beautiful ideas. But a great deal of time passed before humans were able to sail on ships or fly on charter flights. Progress occurred in steps, sometimes large and sometimes very small, and many generations were born and died before these wonderful dreams became a reality. If an ancient inventor had taken their visionary idea to some wealthy chieftain and asked for money to build wings or gills, they would probably have been tarred and feathered—or worse.

But even if the poor inventor got what they were after, they would have first had to deal with a huge range of questions, including: What shape is the Earth? What is gravity? How does the human respiratory system work? And, does it hurt when your forehead hits a cloud? What is your idea worth if it has never been tried, you don't thoroughly understand the details of what's involved and you aren't risking anything yourself?

Many investors make it a key principle to never put their money into ideas alone. I often receive letters that sound something like this: "I have an innovative way to earn a billion dollars. I will create a magical sales platform that will be perfect in every way. Are you interested?" I immediately answer, "No, I'm not interested." The idea might really be good, but the creator should first make a bold attempt to implement it and begin learning through trial and error. But when someone sends me only fancy words with nothing to back them up, I don't believe them. If you are so sure of your idea, see if you can make it fly yourself. Or do you lack faith in it? If so, then why ask an investor to take a risk that you, the founder, wouldn't? If your idea means something to you, break open your piggy bank and invest some of your own money. If that's not enough, ask your spouse for their secret stash or turn to a sibling, your in-laws or whomever. If the people closest to you believe in your idea, then you'll doubtlessly derive great pleasure from implementing it. And if they don't, maybe you should reconsider and take a more skeptical and discerning look at it. No investor will be thrilled that someone just wants to have a try at their expense.

Rule:

A cool idea alone is not enough for an investor: you need to show proof that it can work.

Exception:

I sometimes get approached by successful entrepreneurs whom I know well and have worked with before. In such cases, I can agree to invest based only on an idea—if that idea is something I understand and feel strongly about. This is the advantage of successful serial entrepreneurs. Of course, they don't need to learn the basics: they know what to do and how to do it, which frees them up to focus on making the idea into a reality.

But even at this point, a number of factors must line up properly: it is important for me to understand why a successful and respected entrepreneur is coming to me with nothing but a bare idea, whether they have brought all their previous projects to fruition and whether they are really going to devote a significant part of their life to the project under discussion.

As I mentioned earlier, I once put my faith in a bare idea that a serial entrepreneur presented to me on a slip of paper. Of course, I was taken for a ride: the final product turned out to be very different from the original idea and the entrepreneur distanced himself from the project. I ended my association with the project relatively painlessly, but it left a bad taste in my mouth. And you can be sure that every investor has been burned like this and has had to write off many such projects as a loss. Therefore, investors will go over your brilliant idea with a fine-tooth comb. Even a beautiful presentation, charming smile and gung-ho pitch will be no help to you if the project isn't sound.

The Main Takeaway:

A good idea is a hard-won idea. If you are confident in the idea and are ready to devote lots of time to developing it, don't be afraid to leave your comfort zone, work without a salary and even spend your own funds on the project. Investors are more willing to give funding to a team with multiple cuts and bruises on their faces: this is the best sign that the members are confident in their ultimate success and are ready to do whatever it takes to turn the idea into a reality.

4

THE PITCH IS EVERYTHING

HOW TO GET INVESTORS INTERESTED IN YOUR PROJECT

P *remise:*
    You had a good time at a business conference and head home with your head full of useful information. In the elevator, you are joined by a well-known venture capitalist whom you would have almost no chance of meeting under ordinary circumstances. This might be your only shot to grab their attention and interest

them in your project. You have 30 floors in which to make your pitch.

Question:

Where to start?

Answer:

With prep. This conversation must be rehearsed long before the chance meeting takes place. A founder should have a ready pitch in their head at all times, like a prayer that a monk keeps in his heart. Just ad-lib a joke to get the conversation started.

In sending His apostles out into the world to preach, Jesus Christ gave them the following instructions in Mark 13:11: "Whenever you are arrested and brought to trial, do not worry beforehand about what to say. Just say whatever is given you at the time, for it is not you speaking, but the Holy Spirit."

Without trying to get into a long discussion about heavenly forces, I would say only that in the case of venture investors, this approach definitely won't work—perhaps because they do not hold the power of life and death over startup founders. At worst, investors can only deny them money.

A pitch is a short story about a project that should convince those to whom it is addressed. There are different types of pitches, but we will discuss the investment pitch. It should be both brief and informative, listing what you want to do, the nature of the project, how it is better than others, why it must be implemented and what economic, social and existential effect it will have.

You should neither underestimate or overestimate the value of the pitch. A weak pitch could easily kill your chances of success, even if the project itself is good. But if the project is weak, then even the most brilliant pitch can't save it: professionals will always see right through your empty words. A flashy but hollow pitch might work on sucker investors, but for serious folk, a slick line such as, "The competition won't know what hit 'em! Here's my account number—when can I expect the money?" simply won't work. So don't even bother trying. Sometimes investors do get taken in by such hype but they pay for it later.

As for less potentially tragic situations—that is, when the project really does have merit—the question of focus is key. The pitch must state the gist of the project clearly. To formulate it, you first need to organize your thoughts and have a clear vision of your core competencies and competitive advantages. Here is an example of how *not* to do it. "Check this out: we have come up with a way to exchange information between patients, hospitals, social insurance offices, voluntary health insurance companies and government agencies. This enables you to undergo medical tests and track your medical history. We can also tack on a system for making doctor's appointments. What's more, our technology is very well suited to other markets such as beauty salons, gas stations and travel agencies."

Such pitches typically make my head spin and my eyes twitch as I try to understand the project's main idea.

Rule:

If a person cannot make a focused pitch, he or she will not be able to make a focused project. A weak pitch indicates that the idea has not been thought out thoroughly.

For those who are shy about selling themselves or think it might be overly arrogant to ask strangers for money, I will share a little secret: investors respond to strong, well-honed, focused and clearly worded pitches the same way cats respond to catnip. They like the excitement, the euphoria and the challenge it elicits. This happens to me all the time, and my investment team even tries to hold me back. But I continue considering projects pitched to me on the fly simply because many of these investments have paid off handsomely. My team still tends to get a little nervous about these ventures, so I usually support such projects exclusively out of my own pocket, as an angel investor.

Question from a Timid Startup Founder:

Can you really pitch a project during an elevator ride? Isn't that too pushy?

Wouldn't it be worse to miss the opportunity to get funding for your project and thereby leave a hole in the universe? If you are certain that what you are doing is wonderful and right, then you should have no doubt. This is what is meant by the term *elevator pitch*. When you have a well-honed pitch, you just pull it out of your head and say, "I have a project in which I have absolute confidence. It is both simple and useful. We have invented a new type of baby food that, thanks to its additives, is completely non-allergenic for children under one year of age. This opens up a market for us of $90 billion in New York alone. We can capture 10 percent of the overall market within three years and copycat products cannot appear earlier than in five years. Thus, with an investment of $500,000, the project can bring in $50 million in three years."

If the investor likes it, they will say, "Hmm, I'm interested. Call me tomorrow morning—I'd like to continue this conversation." After that, they will invite you to meet, and if you don't disappoint them, they will write you a check. Of course, at the meeting you'll have to be just as detail-oriented and focused as you were in the elevator.

As a rule, when you don't have a polished pitch, your presentation and materials are vague. This makes it very difficult to communicate with potential investors. This isn't because they are big fans of fine literature but because they know that if you can't convey the gist of your project in 20 seconds, you simply have nothing to say.

The Main Takeaway:

An elevator pitch conveys the gist of your project and why it is economically attractive. Boil it down to a couple of sentences and rehearse it until you can rattle it off automatically.

5

HOW MUCH MONEY TO ASK FOR —AND WHEN

THE REFUELING RULE

Premise:
    With great effort, you manage to put something viable together. The business begins to take shape. Your garage is becoming cramped, but you still don't have enough money to rent an office. Luckily, you happen to meet an angel investor at a bar who is visiting from out of town. After some heavy drinking and your inebriated pitch, they're ready to invest in your project. The angel

will be in town for another couple of days, after which they'll fly back to the cloud they call home and you'll never see them again. All they want in return is a 50 percent share of the business.

Question:

Should you take their check before they gets sober? After all, when will you get this lucky again?

Answer:

Are you certain this visiting business angel doesn't have horns growing from the top of their head?

Let's start with what we have already learned: smart investors do not like obtaining large shares of a business that is still in its early stages because it dampens the team's motivation and changes the nature of its interaction with the investor. But in any case, you need to understand one simple thing: the longer you can go without the help of investment, the higher the price you can charge for even a small share in the company. Therefore, if you understand clearly where you are headed and how you will get there, try to go as long as possible without seeking outside investment. And don't jump at the first offer. At the same time, you need to be careful not to miss the moment when an infusion of cash becomes necessary.

How do you know when this magical moment has arrived? I call it the "car refueling rule."

Rule:

For investors, the best situation is like finding a race car or rocket ship in perfect working order, and all that is needed to make it race or fly is an infusion of fuel. The same is true of startups, with the "fuel" being investment funds. Once you fill the tank, it can tear down the road—or soar to the heavens.

Exception:

I usually reject projects that ask for a lot of money to put together a team and begin making their product—unless the pitch just knocks me out. But as an early-stage investor, I prefer it when the founder has already assembled the team, produced a prototype of some sort, probed the market and made the necessary calculations concerning the probable cost of obtaining customers, how much they can earn from each, how soon they can pay back the investment and so on. In other words, the business model is clear, the unit economics are working and the project can be scaled up. All that remains is to pour gas into the tank. Of course, this is an ideal situation and exactly what a professional investor wants most to see. But even an amateur angel with a modicum of business sense needs to see something before opening his or her checkbook. Otherwise, the investor might simply be drunk. But even then, he or she will eventually sober up and want to see the details.

The next question is how much money to ask for. There is no one-size-fits-all answer to this, but I like to set the goal of financing the project for 18 months into the future. This is because it takes about six months to raise the project to new heights, at which point you will set further goals to achieve. Therefore, limiting your funding horizon to just six months is nerve-racking. Having enough money to last you a year gives you a little breathing room, but having enough for a year and a half is perfect. It allows you to focus on the process without worrying that money will run out tomorrow and force you to lay off staff. It gives you enough time to reach even greater heights and conduct the next round of investment with an even better evaluation.

How can you value a startup that is still so new it has no financial indicators? It is a function of how comfortable both sides are with the project's current condition and its future prospects. Another factor is the volume of the market that it plans to enter.

A proud founder of a small startup once came to me with a high valuation of his project that he claimed would grow rapidly and capture market share. But when I crunched the numbers, it became clear that, at most, the company might double in value—and only if by some magical means it managed to become a monopoly. Of course, we did not give him any money at all.

The valuation should reflect the project's current stage and prospects. Giving away a majority stake for a meager check would, of course, be disastrous. On the other hand, overinflating the value is also risky, so it's a double-edged sword. For example, if you have valued the company at $5 million and during the next round of investment a year later the value is set at only $2 million, questions might arise as to whether everything is kosher with the project or if you cheated someone early on.

In general, a "down round"—that is, raising funds at a lower valuation than the previous round—is extremely stressful for the project and investors. Overinflated initial valuations cause many projects to later collapse.

Of course, everyone wants to place the highest possible value on their brainchild, but even at the first round, you need to be thinking about the second. Don't forget that business is more like a marathon than a sprint.

Rule:

When the valuation of a project grows in steady increments, investors know that everything is going according to plan. But when it fluctuates wildly, doubts and distrust arise.

The Main Takeaway:

Agree on a value that enables the project to develop, motivates the team and gives the investor hope of a profitable exit.

6

MAKING YOUR ENTREPRENEURIAL PLANS

AS BANAL AND ESSENTIAL AS THE AIR YOU BREATHE

Premise:
You have a good product that is simple, clear and in demand. Its functionality effectively solves a limited range of tasks with nothing superfluous and that's why people love it. But new

companies are appearing on the market that have come up with interesting features that, although unrelated to your core competencies, would look good in a package with them. And most importantly, you have accumulated enough spare cash to quickly develop similar solutions.

Question:
Will you develop these wonderful new features before others manage to use them to make all the money in the world?

Answer:
Unfortunately (or fortunately?), nobody can earn all the money in the world. And losing focus could send your own company straight to its grave.

A startup has limited resources, and it is impossible to be the best at everything right from the start. It sometimes seems that business is very straightforward and has an obvious set of rules and formulas that would be impossible to ignore. But I frequently see talented young people and older, experienced business people repeatedly make the same mistakes. Therefore, it is good to review the basic checkpoints for building your entrepreneurial plans.

The first one is the simplest. Ask yourself: I am a startup founder, so what am I creating? Am I introducing a new technology that will change everything, or am I simply taking something that already exists and making it faster, higher and stronger? At this stage, you need to answer this question for yourself very clearly and, most importantly, honestly to avoid falling victim to fantasy, denial and megalomania.

Second, you need to understand your target audience and answer the question of where you are going. You need to visualize your idea as a business. If you imagine that you have only to make your product and everyone will come to you, showering you with praise and money, then you are making an error that is as obvious as it is insidious. This will never happen: even a bar of gold cannot sell itself. Therefore, if you do not understand who your product is designed for and who will buy it, you won't even be able to give it away.

Objection from a Freebie Lover:
What do you mean "you won't be able to give it away"? Everyone loves a freebie!

Reply to the Objection:
People only love freebies that they actually need. Consider Uber: initially, the company invested enormous resources in giving away free trips to build up a customer base. That first free trip was simply a hook: the main thing was knowing whom to hook and how to catch them. The whole art of giving something away for free is that it should quickly lead to monetization.

This is why *freemium* (in which the basic product or service is free but additional functions are paid) and *try-and-buy* (in which you try something for free, but must buy it if you want to continue using it) are so widespread.

For the next question, ask yourself: what kind of business am I building? Your answer determines the type of business model you use. I need to economize my resources and enter the market quickly. Unlike a large corporation, I cannot afford to go through a long development cycle, pour major resources into the project and wait for a long-term result. Therefore, I must focus on my core competence. And, because this is my main competitive advantage, I must understand it clearly and emphasize it.

It is often necessary to explain to startup teams that if they decide to make a multifunctional product and market it to many different types of customers, the project will lose focus and become expensive. My advice is that it's good to aim for high sales, but keep in mind that this is a startup and you would have to spend a lot of money to add all those bells and whistles. And why do we spend it? Because you're trying to do everything at once. As a result, you lack a clearly defined market position. And without that, consumers don't know what you're selling.

Rule:

Without a clear understanding of your core competence, it is impossible to position yourself on the market—and no amount of money can help you in this regard. In fact, having too much money can even cloud the picture and blur the reality of how things really stand.

From this simple and banal rule follows another that is no less simple and clear: you must have the strongest possible team to develop your project's core competence. But there are still many different things that you have to manage for your product to work. So write this advice on a large banner and hang it over the door to your office. *The company doesn't need to do everything itself: outsource everything you can, at least until the initial growth stage is finished.*

This is my deep conviction. I have seen numerous founders crippled by problems that arose because they refused to heed this advice from the start. And despite ignoring my warnings, two months into the business, they came back asking for more money. I would tell them, "No, I won't give any more. You can do what you want, but I won't finance it. You think you understand everything and can do everything yourself, but everything you've done has failed. And by digging your heels in, you stubbornly refuse outside help. I don't play that way."

Rule:

At the growth stage, outsource everything unrelated to your core competencies. Otherwise, you could become entangled in a mess and sink to the bottom. In some cases, you can also outsource in subsequent stages. For example, Volkswagen kept only engine manufacturing and overall design in-house and delegated everything else to suppliers.

Why is this so important? Because if you want to be successful, you must be focused and offer something that is easy for others to understand. My favorite example of this comes from physics. You can use bang your hand against a wall to try to make a hole in it for days, or else you can use a hammer and a nail. Which will make a hole in the wall faster? Obviously, the nail will because it is thin, sharp and applies much greater pressure per unit of area. A startup that is trying to develop too many competencies is like that hand beating against the wall. As a rule, such companies fail because they lack the necessary focus to accomplish their primary task.

In addition, it is very important to understand that you can't be the best at everything right from the start, that it takes a long time to reach that point. Let's say I have a customer relationship management (CRM) system, but then I decide to tack on a text messaging module, document management systems and a whole host of wonderful things. As a result, even assuming that everything works, we will now be competing against not just one other company, but against multiple companies in each segment for which we have a product. And even if by some miracle we manage to outperform all of them initially, it would prove almost impossible to maintain that lead over the long term. This is because new solutions and new technologies are constantly appearing and your competitors will all develop in different directions, making it that much harder to somehow keep up with them.

By the way, this applies to large businesses as much as it does to small ones. What makes entrepreneurial projects of any size successful is their focus on root competencies, and those competencies are what drive their rise to the very top. When a project receives a lot of funding, it can start doing some secondary things on its own, but savvy founders always keep their sights focused squarely on the core competencies, changing or replacing side projects as the situation demands. This gives you the freedom to choose only the best solutions at all times. The main thing is to not lose focus and to only shift your attention to the various add-ons when there is no risk of losing a key competitive advantage and the project's main message.

You should also avoid getting distracted by taking orders for various types of side projects. This can happen when a team has attracted little or no funding at the start. The project is growing and has big plans, but an outside player suddenly appears and says, "This looks great, but could you make me the same thing with buttons made of pearl on it?" The team thinks, "Well, our solution is almost complete. We can do this side project, earn some much-needed cash and then incorporate the change into our original design."

Of course, this is nothing but self-delusion and a loss of focus that threatens to turn the project into a service company. What happens when a startup allows itself to get distracted by side projects? A number of large clients appear and, at some point, the company discovers that their development and support department has grown much larger. Why? Because it is carrying out several very different tasks at the same time—everything from pearl buttons for one company to pink bows for another. And even though they are all in the same general field, the individual tasks are completely different. A system integrator at an established corporation could pull it off, first because it would take more money for the job, and second because it has a structure tailored specifically for this. In fact, they do not develop most of these things themselves, but gather them from what is already available on the market. But if a startup has only just taken its first steps and then allows itself to be pulled in different directions, it is certain to go nowhere. The typical argument in favor of taking this path is that it would be crazy to turn down the chance to work for a big-name client. But the project becomes seriously disoriented as a result, the team begins losing its technological lead and is forced to admit that it no longer has a firm grip on its core competencies. At this point, additional players appear on the scene who can do the same thing just as well as your project can, meaning that you are no longer the leader, but just one of several players on the market. And even worse, you have run out of money.

An Uber Driver's Objection:

But what about Uber? The company was once an alternative taxi service and now also delivers food. Uber seems to be doing just fine, despite this blurring of its focus.

Reply to This Objection:

No, this is not a blurring of its focus, but the introduction of additional monetization channels based on its core competence. Uber's business model is built on attracting freelance drivers. That is what they do, and the fact that those drivers sometimes deliver food instead of passengers does not change the basic idea. And, with a billion dollars in capitalization, Uber has begun including additional channels of monetization —something that would take a startup years to accomplish.

The next important point concerns the geographic focus of your project. Are you out to conquer the whole world? If so, do you understand the promotional methods and psychology in different countries? Are you hoping to simply hammer your app together, post it in the AppStore and then sit poolside while the whole world eagerly snatches up this treasure you've created? Unfortunately, that's not going to happen. You need to have primary markets in which you will succeed. If you have managed to build up a strong customer base in, say, North America and Germany, but you've also gained a few users in China and Indonesia, then hats off to you—but that smattering of users appeared independently of your efforts because you devoted no resources to attracting them. The goal is to succeed where you have chosen to devote your resources. For this reason, I always look very carefully at the markets and the possibility of gradually scaling up to the global level. And in this regard, it is very important to understand that a project created in one context can also succeed in similar settings. If you reshape the project for every attractive market you find, it will turn into a hodgepodge of different micro-projects that no one will perceive as a coherent whole.

Founders frequently make the mistake of thinking that once they've honed everything to perfection on the home market, it will be simple to achieve the same success globally. Although you might be able to easily transition between such similar markets as Germany and Austria or Canada and the US, in other cases you are probably just wasting your time. Investors will not buy into this mistaken assumption and will expect to see a proof of concept in the target market.

The next point concerns three magic letters: KPI (key performance indicators). Typically, KPIs measure a company's success against a set of targets and milestones. Common performance indicators are: revenue growth, revenue per client, profit margin, client retention rate, and customer satisfaction. We always demand that the project has a clear and understandable plan along with metrics to help us analyze success. People constantly ask why this is necessary considering that frequently, the plan described at the early stage is just bullshit and never turns out the way the founder imagined anyway. I answer this question by paraphrasing Peter the Great: "The boyars should express themselves in writing, so that everyone's stupidity is evident." The written word is much stronger than speech alone. If you don't see the need to do the math and make projections, you will most likely produce complete garbage. The moment someone begins working out their projection in detail, however, they uncover such huge mistakes that they realize they must revise their whole approach. Unlike a quick sketch on a greasy restaurant napkin, a table of figures forces you to discipline your thinking.

Additionally, don't let your first success make you cocky. If the project has gotten off to a good start, it only means you could fall from an even greater height later on and that you are now even more obligated to work with the most prosaic of numerical indicators. The budget and sales plan are the law by which the company will live for the next quarter, year and decade. In fact, all of this is similar to a microstate: the soundness of the basic figures and how well their dynamics are understood determine the soundness and legitimacy of the leader. The team adopts a budget, monitors progress, makes adjustments for emergencies and sets goals.

Of course, we are not talking about the type of various accounting tricks that give detailed descriptions and copies of receipts for pencils and antidepressants. But you should definitely have goals: if you don't have motivators such as a desired number of users, conversions and recoverability projections, then how do you hope to accomplish anything? What's more, KPIs are an excellent indicator of investment suitability for the next round. Let's say that our company is preparing to stage a major round of investment. "Okay," we say, "we've got sales of $3 million and an annual growth rate of 70 percent, but to stage a major round of investment we need $10 million in sales and a growth rate of more than 100 percent. That's our goal." We then identify the resources needed to achieve it and go for it!

The Main Takeaway:

Focus, focus, focus! Keep your sights on the main product, your primary customers, the main market and the project's key indicators.

7

A GEOLOGIST, AN IDEOLOGIST AND SOME REAL SAD SH*T

THE FIRST LAW OF ENTREPRENEURSHIP

P *remise:*
You have a business that received funding four years ago. The idea turned out to be pretty good and some people are even using your product. The company has yet to become a unicorn, but you have enough money for all your operating costs and even enough to live a quiet, comfortable life. The business remains at a nice plateau, with no major ups or downs. Should you now think about developing your inner self and taking up meditation? Isn't this great?

Question:
What does your investor think about the business?
Answer:
If they do bother thinking about it at all anymore, they probably refer to it as a "lifestyle business"—meaning some "real sad shit."

Didn't we agree to talk straight? My intention is not to point fingers at anyone. Businesses differ, and if a business has found enough backing to launch, it means someone—perhaps only the founder and his or her family—needed or wanted it. But for an investor, a business that manages only to stay afloat is the worst possible option. You might think investors fear failure and losing money most of all. That isn't true. Failures are perfectly normal and unavoidable. Investors calmly accept the fact that some projects will succeed and others will fail. But it is very difficult for investors to come to terms with "lifestyle businesses" that hover interminably between life and death. Sadly, I have several such businesses in my portfolio right now.

What's so bad about a "lifestyle business"? Let's say we have invested in a project that has stopped growing but earns enough money to pay the team members. At this point, the entrepreneur might think, "Is this so bad? I pay taxes, feed my family and pay our employees on time. Yes, we've hit a plateau, but at least we haven't crashed and we've made a lot of people happy."

It's true that the entrepreneur is earning enough to pay their bills, but in all of this, has anyone thought about the investor? What should they do? They know they shouldn't pump more money into the business and yet they can't make a decent exit from it either. The project gets stashed away in a dusty attic, like a suitcase without a handle. When a company goes bankrupt, you walk away and forget about it. If a company grows as hoped, you sell it. But what to do with a business that does neither? It seems to be working, yet nobody will buy it. You sit on the board of directors with nothing to do: you can't walk away from the business, and you don't earn any dividends from it, either.

An entrepreneur should strive for great things. Of course, projects that generate little profit also have a right to exist—to which their great number testifies. But these are not venture projects.

In fact, an investment fund brings together various people's money and takes on projects with a time limit in mind. That is, a venture capital investment fund should eventually exit each project at a profit to return money to investors. But this is impossible with "lifestyle businesses," and that's why investors hate them. Such businesses essentially take your money to finance a good life for their employees, but for no one else. In return, you get from them only a basket of fruit and a postcard from the Maldives saying "Wish you were here."

Rule:

Constant growth, both creative and financial, is what it means to be an entrepreneur. You can't help but strive for progress and innovation and will risk everything to achieve it. If, however, you have gotten stuck at a certain point and feel okay with that, then don't delude yourself: you are not an entrepreneur, but someone who has taken early retirement.

Exceptions:

There are no exceptions to this rule!

The "lifestyle business" phenomenon is not specific to particular countries, personal backgrounds or even climates. Such businesses—and the people who like them—are found everywhere in roughly the same proportion. It's just that, by nature, some people are born entrepreneurs and some are not. And in a capitalist system, the entrepreneur is the central figure who makes the world spin and transform under the influence of both good and bad entrepreneurial ideas.

I once studied political economy at a university. It was an incomprehensible subject with an equally perplexing name. It taught us that under feudalism or capitalism, the landowner or person holding the means of production is king. My experience, however, suggests that just the opposite is true, especially with regard to modern capitalism. You might possess substantial means of production and huge tracts of land, but by themselves, they are dormant resources. You can't do anything with them until you have a viable business idea. What's more, you probably have to pay a hefty sum for maintenance and taxes on these "assets." An entrepreneur is the person with the idea and the will to make it happen. He or she understands how to improve things and how to create revolutionary new products that no one else has envisioned—products that win a place on the market once they appear. An entrepreneur is never at rest, but constantly looks for opportunities and ways to exploit them.

This is why I believe that entrepreneurism is not a type of activity but a character trait. An entrepreneur is inclined to create, whether it is an ordinary business, socially responsible business, progressive community service, breakthrough in fundamental science or something else. Leonardo da Vinci, Nikola Tesla, and Albert Einstein were all entrepreneurs, although, of course, they never formed legal entities akin to a modern business. In today's context, an entrepreneur is someone who is at their best when creating new commercial enterprises. Note the close connection between the words *entrepreneur* and *enterprise*. An entrepreneur is someone who can create an enterprise and then lead it to success.

A Manager's Objection:

Have you ever seen these disheveled-looking geniuses who can never find their eyeglasses or a pair of matching socks because their thoughts are so focused on lofty matters?

Reply to the Objection:

Yes, and it is very important to understand that dreaming up something new and managing its production are two very different functions. Entrepreneurs often make lousy managers, but they needn't be reborn as good ones. Instead, they can bring in experienced professionals to manage the enterprise.

Rule:

Most successful startups are led by two figures: the original entrepreneur and a strong manager. A good example is Google, where the founders brought in Eric Schmidt to take the helm.

Exceptions:

Exceptions are rare, but they do happen. Perhaps the most striking is Steve Jobs, who managed his business well, albeit not perfectly. He created Apple and made it into a powerhouse, even though his own management eventually kicked him out. Still, he is an exception. It is much more common for professional managers to step in and put all the operational processes in order. The entrepreneur is like a life-giving bacterium that gets things going and keeps them moving, whereas managers are like a preservative agent for stabilizing operations.

This leads to a question: Where is the investor in all this? They seem to be focused on the future and the big picture, but aren't they also concerned about profits, legal issues and other such matters?

I see the investor as a subspecies of entrepreneur who, having evaluated a set of business ideas, can understand which are more promising and worth financing. In other words, an investor is an entrepreneur—and then some. They have crystallized the essence of their business and entrepreneurial experience and now work strictly with ideas. They are like a geologist looking for gold. Once an investor has gained some experience, connections and a good reputation, he or she receives a large stream of project proposals that must be understood, categorized, and either discarded ruthlessly or seized post haste. My greatest strength is knowing how to size up an entrepreneur and their idea, as well as their ability to bring that idea to fruition.

The Main Takeaway:

Set global goals and strive to create the very best products and technologies possible. Every successful venture project is based on the prospect of making revolutionary changes.

8

THE GLITTER AND THE MISERY OF UNIT ECONOMICS

FINDING THE BALANCE BETWEEN GROWTH AND PROFITABILITY

P *remise:*
    You came up with a business and found a very willing investor. You soon learned to cover all of your operating expenses, reached the break-even point and, a little later, began turning a tidy profit. For several months now, you've been steadily collecting your 15

percent off the top. Now, the business isn't growing, but it isn't shrinking either. You happily inform the investor of the good news.
Question:
How will the investor react to this wonderful news?
Answer:
Most likely, they will breathe heavily into the phone for a while, then croak ominously, "Unit economics!"

This is a very important topic that few people consider. What are unit economics?

Unit economics are usually defined as a method of economic modeling used to determine the profitability of a business model by evaluating the profitability of a unit of goods or a single customer. More simply, unit economics is the ratio of the cost of attracting a client to the projected income from that client over time.

When we talk about a classic business, we naturally think in terms of profit. A startup, however, is different in that growth and scalability are much more important, and the question of profit can be put on the back burner for quite some time.

When a startup becomes profitable, there is a critical need for explosive growth. You must urgently kick the investor in the shins and say, "It's time to spend money on scaling and development." Experienced investors know that it is extremely rare for a business to achieve significant growth after only a single infusion of funds. Let's say I have sales of $100,000 and expenses of $80,000. That shows a profit, but the investor expected to earn a significant return on the investment. How far will that $20,000 in profit get you if the investor sank $1 million into the project? Comparing income and expenses is only half of the job. The other half is to deliver your product to customers and to get them to come back for your product again and again. For a startup, the second task is much more important than the first.

Let's say a startup grows by 10 percent per month but remains unprofitable overall due to administrative expenses that are dragging it down. Is this so bad? Of course not! As soon as it can achieve healthy unit economics and put channels in place for attracting new customers, sales will increase and that will erase all these other problems. The main goal is to earn multiple returns on the cost of attracting each customer—and the sooner the better.

In the language of chess, you make a tactical sacrifice. By giving up some pawns to your opponent, you initially seem to be at a disadvantage, but you've gained a strategic advantage in the process that ultimately enables you to win the game. And when you have the satisfaction of putting your opponent in checkmate, you won't shed any tears for the pawns you sacrificed earlier. After all, the real prize here is the king, not some lowly pawns.

Rule:

At the startup stage, the growth rate is much more important than short-term profits. With the right approach to unit economics, the financial returns from high-quality, rapid growth exceed basic expenses many times over.

In the early stages, you might fail to identify the best distribution channels and burn through all your money without managing to achieve "free flight." Nevertheless, a startup needs to do these things to make itself seen and heard without worrying too much yet about the costs involved and unit economics. Uber is one of the most famous examples of a modern business that initially paid much more for each client than it earned. Despite the enormous cost of attracting clients and the general unprofitability of the business at that early stage, everyone involved understood that they would have to burn through piles of cash before things could start coming up roses. To this day, though, those flowers have yet to bloom.

A very telling recent case was the failure of the WeWork IPO. In pursuit of rapid growth and a 12-digit valuation at the IPO, the company decided to forego profitable unit economics, wagering that since the market had forgiven Uber this short-coming, WeWork could get away with it also. They were wrong. The market judged the company harshly, dashing its hopes for an IPO, prompting the founder to abandon the project and driving the valuation down to only a 10-digit figure. Although this might seem good for some projects, in this case it meant a tenfold drop from its valuation in the previous round of investment.

I have dealt with several projects that demonstrate how one should and shouldn't work with unit economics. Let's begin with a less than successful case. There is one very good project that we have not taken on but persistently invites us to join. This startup has used new technologies to sell women's under-wear. Everything about it is cool—the AI, customization and excellent brand perception. In short, it's not just a business, but a fairy tale.

However, when we took a closer look we discovered that the company spends $50 to attract each client and recoups that cost only after the third sale. The problem is: how soon does that third sale take place? In this business, the client returns, at best, only once every six months and, at worst, only once a year or not at all. The upshot: the project is unprofitable. Still, I didn't care about that. What bothered me was that the unit economics were unfavorable, and that overcoming this hurdle would require an investment of tens of millions of dollars—a sum that, of course, no one would give them. I saw no other way to conquer this market and attract the number of customers this project would need to become profitable.

Here is a more upbeat example.

One of our successful projects started by selling condoms to women by subscription. The business was developing well, but there was no ongoing customer demand. As useful as condoms are, women don't need them on a regular basis: they might need one urgently today, but tomorrow—who knows? The result was that this founder, a woman herself, had a great brand focused on women, a growing business, but unstable unit economics.

At this point, she had a brilliant insight into the problem and decided to turn the project around. What did she realize? To ensure regular profits, she altered the business model slightly to offer subscription purchases of tampons and pads— the frequency and regularity of demand for which can be predicted almost perfectly. She had already put her audience and brand in place and simply added modern, high-quality products that are in constant demand. The ratio of the cost of attracting each client to the income from each client improved dramatically. After this, the business really took off and we soon sold it for an excellent price to the world leader in this niche.

In conclusion, it is worth noting that unit economics affect how often customers buy your product and also the cost of production of attracting each client. During the limited promotional period at the beginning, you can afford to spend more making your product than you earn from selling it, but you will inevitably reach the point where you conclude that the market price should cover production costs. From then on, you either operate in the black or your business fails miserably.

Rule:

The ratio of the cost of attracting a client and what that client will spend on your product over time is the most important characteristic of any project. The more you can recoup costs, the higher your chances of success and rapid growth.

The Main Takeaway:

Many entrepreneurs do not take unit economics into account, which leads to much floundering about and, in most cases, money lost and the project's collapse. Investors want to see that projects have the best possible unit economics.

9

HEAD-SPINNING SUCCESS

WHEN VICTORY IS FAR MORE CHALLENGING THAN FAILURE

P *remise:*

Let's suppose your business isn't going well and you can barely manage to make ends meet when, by some amazing coincidence, you win the lottery and become rich. Newspapers that had never noticed you before suddenly want an interview to learn how you plan to spend your incredible fortune.

Question:

It's great, huh? Your life will definitely be better and happier now, right?

Answer:

In all likelihood, no. In fact, life might even get worse.

Of course, someone winning the lottery and an entrepreneur striking it rich are two very different things, but bear with me for a minute. Imagine how hard it would be for someone who had always lived paycheck to paycheck to suddenly find themselves swimming in money. What should they do with it? How to keep oneself and one's money safe? How to keep the surge of borrowers at bay? How do you keep from losing your head knowing that you can suddenly buy almost everything you want, whereas only a few days before, you had almost nothing? If the lucky entrepreneur lacks inner fortitude, financial literacy and restraint, this gift of fate might be more like a hurricane that rips through their old life and leaves everything in ruins. It remains a very serious question as to whether they will manage to adapt to this new state of affairs or will simply be overcome by it.

Now let's get back to our bullish business. When a project starts to grow, it faces numerous dangers with which many businesses fail to cope. Why? Just imagine: a startup begins with, say, five employees and then it starts growing, adding a huge number of clients very rapidly, with the result that the original staff of five swells to 50, 100 or even 1,000 employees. At this point, the founder suddenly discovers that it is necessary to put a whole system in place for managing people and finances in a completely different way. The problem is that the disheveled genius who was fueled by inspiration and who could live on potato chips and Coca-Cola while they and three friends stayed up nights cobbling something together in the garage is not necessarily cut out to an be organized and systematic manager of a large team of people. When a project enters the phase of unexpected success, the founders must have fortitude. Your business is always a reflection of your personality, and if it starts to grow, you will inevitably have to grow, too—and this, by the way, is painful. A successful project requires that a leader have new competencies that they usually lack, that they follow a new way of life that they generally resist and that they change their outlook and reassess their values. Different founders cope with these challenges differently: some calmly readjust and strengthen their team while others go off the deep end, suffering from insomnia, panic, and constant doubt. The psychological pitfalls of sudden success have brought down countless promising projects.

Rule:

If you plan to succeed, then prepare for success. It is better to build up your managerial skills in advance and have at least a general plan of action in place in case everything goes well.

In addition to the psychological side of the business, there is also a financial side: when the project starts growing rapidly, you need to maintain the pace, buy more and more traffic, attract customers, find funds to support the process and develop the product. Which means, you can suddenly run into a cash crunch. These are normal growing pains for a business.

If you experience these symptoms, don't worry. You are definitely not the first to have them and they can be overcome. If you calmly and deliberately change and strengthen the team, then everything can go smoothly. But if you stress out, the task will be much harder. And you need to be mentally prepared for the fact that someone will have to fire and hire new people, withstand pressure from all sides and ward off doubt.

This advice might sound odd, but when you get the time, watch the HBO series *Silicon Valley*. *It does* a pretty good job of depicting the specific aspects of our industry and the lifecycle of a startup. In one episode, the founder unexpectedly comes into $10 million, causing him to have panic attacks. This is not far-fetched at all: I have seen even worse happen to founders under similar circumstances. And this has nothing to do with personal weakness or frailty, nor is it germane to the ultra-wealthy. Just imagine if an enormous responsibility were thrust upon you: any misstep could spell disaster, and competitors who never even noticed you before were now watching your every move. Plus, you would need to maintain communication with the venture capital funds and investors who were backing you. It would be like if you had won the lottery, with your phone ringing off the hook as dozens of distant relatives call with requests to help them solve their difficult problems. The difference is that, with the lottery, you are only responsible for maintaining your own psychological health and your winnings, but with a startup, everything is much more complicated and potentially tragic.

We frequently encounter such situations in our line of work. We tend to forget that we need to be able to cope not only with very bad situations but also with very good ones. The truth is: neither type is easy. And although in business they say, "This is a good problem to have," the transition to the growth stage requires a change in the management model, formalization of the business processes and proper budget management.

. . .

The Main Takeaway:

Early on, bring strong managers onto your team who know how to respond to positive but difficult challenges.

10

A FEW WORDS ON VESTING

HANDSHAKES ONLY WORK IN PRISON OR ON THE PLAYGROUND

P *remise:*
    You and a friend create a startup and split the shares in the company 50-50. It is tough at first: you eat nothing but instant noodles, borrow money wherever you can and work through the nights. But still, nothing is working out. One day, when the project seems dead in the water, your friend announces that they can't take it anymore and is leaving for Bali to rest and recuperate. However, out of sheer obstinacy, you keep pounding your head against the wall. About a year later, a miracle occurs: you are suddenly noticed and the company begins to grow by leaps and bounds. At this moment, your friend who owns half the company suddenly appears at your door with an enigmatic smile on their face.

Question:
What will you tell your friend?
Answer:
"Hi." There is nothing more to say because, as the legal owner of half the company, they have the right to smile as wide as they want.

Sometimes I think people actually like to repeat the mistakes of their predecessors. How else to explain why people so energetically and enthusiastically sign up for the school of hard knocks? In the case of the exhausted friend who took off for Bali, as a parting gift, the other founder should have first presented them with a revised contract to sign, one that lays out new conditions for their partnership.

Let's say we decided to create a project and divided the shares equally. We shook hands on it and off we went. We couldn't have been happier taking those initial steps together, but after a month, one of us has lost their enthusiasm. It gets even crazier when a project has multiple shareholders and it reaches the point at which only one of them is doing any work: the rest are simply sipping martinis and waiting for cash to rain down from heaven.

To prevent such situations from arising, use a vesting mechanism. To put it simply, when a person joins a project as an employee or partner, or when the project attracts investments, set up a timeline that incentivizes their on-going participation.

For example, an owner tells you, "Yes, we agreed to give you a certain number of shares, but for now, your shares are not yours. They will become yours as you continue working for the company. We want you to devote four years to this, and after completing each year you will receive another 25 percent of your shares. You asked us to invest money in you, and you need to return the favor somehow." If this person decides to leave after one year, they will own one-fourth of his shares, and if they leave after two years, they will own one-half of the total. The rest of the shares will remain at the disposal of the company, which will have the option of using them to attract employees who will actually develop the business.

Vesting is also common when it comes to public workers and their pensions. Working at the DMV or as a public school teacher is hard and sometimes thankless work. So, how are people incentivized to keep showing up for work every day? Labor unions along with government agencies offer a generous pension plan for employees once they retire—only after they have been toiling for five years. After five years, they are vested in the pension program. Quit after only four years? You get nothing.

I consider vesting a very healthy practice that protects projects from various types of unpleasantness. It is very much in keeping with the mechanism for obtaining options.

An Indignant Co-founder's Objection:
What the heck?! Gentlemen don't act this way!

Response to the Objection:
Unfortunately, there is always the possibility that, at some early stage of the business, someone will ignore the rules of good form and violate verbal agreements—even if they were sealed with blood. This is a major stumbling block for almost all businesses. Entrepreneurs thump their chests in indignation saying, "Don't you respect me? Why should I give you my shares? They're already mine," and so on. And this happens over and over again. Better to hash out these details in advance, rather than regret the oversight later.

Rule:

Blood pacts are better for schoolchildren and thieves than for business people. Unfortunately, morality and ethics are often forgotten when large sums of money are at stake. It is better to employ vesting early on than it is to lose a friend, or worse, see that friend become an enemy.

Exception:

Although rare, sometimes everyone involved in the process is happy to use vesting and don't make a scene about it. The savviest entrepreneurs—who have all been burned in the past —know how difficult and unpleasant it is to try to dilute the share of a business partner who is sabotaging the business and will gladly use vesting to avoid the fallout that comes from broken promises.

Is vesting a sign of rudeness or distrust? Not from the point of view of the industry, but opinions differ. Some entrepreneurs see it as a personal insult. I have encountered this reaction on several occasions and even agreed to proceed without vesting because I was closely acquainted with the team and had discussed all the risks with them in detail. Everything turned out well in the end, but in hindsight, it would still have been better to include vesting.

Why did I decide to touch on this sensitive issue? Because I really want these basic norms in place at the industry level and for them to become customary for everyone. Otherwise, every time I lay the foundation of a business relationship, I have to wade through prickly resentments and wounded egos. To build harmonious motivation for the team, at least some kind of consensus is necessary; an understanding that these are the general rules of the game and not an attempt by one person to assert themselves at another's expense. Far too often, I have faced the idiotic situation of one of the company's main shareholders suddenly giving up on everything, throwing their shares in a suitcase and flying off to Bangkok to smoke weed. I am sincerely surprised by such behavior. Some team members find investors, work through the night and take all the risks while others just kick back on a beach somewhere. And if the business fails? They just send instructions on where to transfer their money.

Maybe elite business schools teach these basic truths, but then why are there so many confused people with severely messed up *capitalization tables*? And I am completely serious in my sniping about elite business schools. A few years ago, I spoke with the founder of a US company for whom I had acted as an angel investor. I saw that the business needed to beef up its technical side and said that we needed to look for a strong technical staff. The bright-eyed founder replied that he had already found a technical director.

"And how did you land him?" I asked.

"I gave him 50 percent of the company," he replied, shrugging his shoulders.

"Listen, kid," I said, "did you graduate from Harvard or an online-only scam program? I'm guessing the latter. Let's sort this out."

The founder quickly understood the problem and confessed. "As a matter of fact," he said, "the new technical director is a flop. He can't do anything."

"I knew from my first conversation with him that he wasn't up to the task and I shared my doubts with you," I said. "But you gave him one-half of the company."

That was how the cookie crumbled. If we had put vesting in place, we could have easily dismissed the inept technical director and moved on. But now, nothing could be done to improve the situation.

The bright-eyed founder replied:

"He's a reasonable guy and won't do anything to harm the company. I'll initiate a round and ask him to sell his share."

And what if he doesn't want to sell? What if he's not so reasonable? And what if he, in fact, wants to harm the company? In situations with lots of "what ifs," something bad inevitably happens. The best thing is to simply install measures that will prevent trouble from happening later, no matter how much it upsets your well-meaning associates.

Though it did nothing for my ego, it turned out that I was right. Now the parties are ending their working relationship and wasting time and money in the process.

The Main Takeaway:

Feel free to talk about vesting. It doesn't restrict anybody's rights. It does, however, guarantee that the project will move forward, even if a particular participant experiences a change of mind or attitude. This is equally important for both the team and the investor.

11

KARMA AND CONVERTIBLE NOTES

WHEN LOVE IS ONLY ONE CHECK AWAY FROM HATE

P *remise:*
You've decided to start a business. You don't have any money, but you do have a best friend with lots of money and no particular

interest in that whole entrepreneurship thing. They're happy to lend you $10,000 with no strings attached and no set deadline: you can repay it once you've earned it. You soon earn a hundred times more and present your best friend with their $10,000 and a bottle of good whiskey.

Question:

Is your friend now an investor with bragging rights?

Answer:

This is your best friend. You can say lots of good things about them, but they are definitely not an investor. All they did was give you the opportunity to turn your idea into reality. They're a good friend, that's all.

How does an investor differ from your mother? Your mother simply loves you without needing anything in return. An investor wants to make money off you—and not two or three percent like a bank would, but preferably much more than they invested. Today's bright young entrepreneurs often have difficulty getting their heads around this simple idea.

This brings us naturally to another investment tool besides shares: convertible notes. This tool is typical at early stages of investment but is rare at later stages.

How does it work?

A convertible note is used to facilitate the investment process—for both the project and investors. The note stipulates that it will be converted into shares at the next round or when it reaches maturity.

The note might also contain a valuation or it could just be a discount for the next round. It is essentially a loan with the right to buy shares.

However, there are some finer points as well.

Let's say that we invest money in your project then sit back and wait while it grows. Then someone comes along and buys you out—or rather, they buy a controlling stake in your company.

A convertible note gives you the right to leave this party and to take your money with a specified premium. After all, an investor does not always want to work with new project managers.

But I had one funny instance when a founder apparently confused me with his mother or best friend. I gave a convertible note as an angel investor without involving the venture capital fund. The company in question was very promising. The business was growing well and all the participants of the process were convinced that the project would raise a second round of investment. Of course, I planned to use that round to convert my note and exit the project with a good profit. But things didn't go according to plan. The company suddenly became profitable without having to raise any more rounds. Yes, it does happen sometimes that an entrepreneur starts out by accumulating convertible notes but manages to avoid sinking into the abyss of financial obligations. And so this entrepreneur decided to buy out all the notes and sell the company. What's more, he found a proviso by which he could return the funds at nearly face value and, in his words, everyone had agreed to this.

When he came to me with this proposal, I said, "Are you crazy? We spent three years with this company and now it has become profitable—congratulations. Let's keep it going. Nobody gave you another round? Then let me give it to you. Let's convert the note." To this, the entrepreneur replied that he didn't need a round, and that everything was fine as it was. After that, I asked what would happen to my money. He said that if I wanted, I could have it back. Very nice of him, right?

What, exactly, was the problem here? The company did not raise a round of investment and was not sold. The convertible note did not clearly state what happens if there is no round, and yet that's exactly what happened. And in response to my objection that this is not the way things are done, I was told to re-examine the fine print. However, everything ended well: it took some time, but I convinced the entrepreneur that what he was doing was wrong—and I didn't use legalese to get my point across. As a result, he bought me out at a more or less fair price and not just for the sum that I had invested.

A Couple of Busybodies:

What do you mean you "didn't use legalese"? Did you take him out back and rough him up, or what?

No, it was nothing like that. In fact, no decent angel investor uses the methods you see in gangster films. I simply made another call—and that's sometimes enough. I basically said, "I supported you from the very start. I was the most reliable among your investors, many of whom came to your project through me. We did everything to get you through the rough times. And now that things are going well, you suddenly take a different tone with us. If you do this, it will have a very bad effect on your karma. After all, life is about more than just a bunch of legal documents."

Speaking of documents, the contract was somewhat subpar because the investment was relatively small. The founder had called me asking for urgent assistance. I said, "Okay, send over the contract. I'll sign it and write you a check." No lawyers or anyone else really looked at it. Because it was an urgent request, I simply hoped the fellow would behave himself. If this deal had not been a personal angel investment, but had gone through my venture capital fund or come through a recommendation, such antics would be shut down. But what happened happened. After that phone call, we continued communicating for a couple of months, at which point he called me and said, "I've thought about it and decided that I don't want to spoil my karma. Let's make an arrangement like you suggested." We did and they paid.

To complete the picture, it is also worth mentioning SAFE (Simple Agreement for Future Equity). This is a form that YCombinator, a startup accelerator, developed and it soon gained wide usage for early-stage investments.

Just remember that SAFE grants no rights at all and guarantees neither shares nor a loan. It is a promise to sell shares in the future. That is, SAFE only comes into play if the project experiences rapid growth—at which point you'll have to fight for the right to invest more and not get left behind as a second-class investor.

Rule:

At every stage of the business relationship, you should remember that one of you is the entrepreneur and the other is the investor. You are not best friends, a mother and son or long lost relatives. And always read what you sign.

Sure, it sounds a bit harsh. After all, the act of creating and working together brings people closer, and it is fair to ask: what place do friendly feelings and empathy have? It seems to me that the investor-entrepreneur relationship often resembles a complicated love affair. First comes the flowers and candy; the period when everything is hunky-dory. Then the business booms and outgrows the investor. At this point, the world's leading investment funds come knocking and the entrepreneur gets very heady and leaves. Sometimes, life knocks them for a loop and they return to the original investor as if nothing had happened and offer to start all over again. Once, a project founder even stopped answering my calls after one of the world's leading investors took an interest in him. Then, when his company was sold for pennies on the dollar, he had the nerve to come to me with a new project, saying that he had always respected me *soooo* much and "couldn't we just forget about the past?"

The Main Takeaway:

The use of simplified investment tools, especially at an early stage, saves everyone time and effort later. But even with these in place, it is important to carefully read the handful of provisions that have a major effect on the project's future profitability.

PART III

CASE STUDIES

1

A GENERAL CASE STUDY

THE PASSION FOR MONETIZATION, OR: PATIENCE, MY DEAR!

I often hear people say, "How can you invest in startups that don't monetize their users? That's just a lot of hype, devoid of economic sense." This is actually a very important question, one that I have repeatedly answered to quell both my own doubts and those of skeptics. But instead of rushing to conclusions, let's consider specific cases.

Consider Instagram, the world's most famous social network for photos. It was created at a time when Flickr already existed and had been acquired by Yahoo. Flickr did not fail to charge for storing photos and was very popular—although Yahoo did not pay a lot of money for it.

Then Instagram came along and let users post photos from their mobile phones. What's so amazing about that? Lots of services let you upload photos for free. But its convenient format and simple photo editing tools made the service wildly popular. Still, it held back from monetizing its users and spent huge sums without bringing in any money.

After difficult negotiations, Zuckerberg paid a ten-figure sum for Instagram, which many saw as an extravagance. But today, Instagram's audience is comparable to Facebook's in terms of monetization and is growing very quickly.

The story with venture capital investors is similar. Yuri Milner offered to invest in Facebook with a valuation of $10 billion even though, at that time, the social network had not yet learned how to make money. Many professionals could not understand why Milner would take such an audacious step. How could the social network overcome its huge losses and start earning serious money from its user base?

But a few years later, Facebook held its first IPO: the shares soared in value and continue to rise today. It became clear to everyone that Milner's math had been correct.

I have seen similar things in my experience. Sometimes, it is very important to take your time without pushing the project to monetize. If you make that move at the wrong moment— before the technological solutions are all in place or when the user base is still incomplete or the product or service for which users would pay is not fully defined—you could wind up disappointing your clients, business partners and investors.

For example, the GuruShots project, an app that allows users to enter into photography contests for exposure and cash prizes, had been working in the photography market for a long time and postponed monetization for several years, until it became clear that users liked the product and were ready to pay for it. That patience has led to steady growth.

OpenWeb has a slightly different story. The project helps any website become its own social network with pop-up chat "Spots" and lets visitors discuss content and the brand without having to leave the page—or the accompanying ads. OpenWeb attracted many of the world's leading media outlets and only two years later, having gathered numerous business partners and built an excellent product, the company began to increase sales rapidly.

There are also some very popular projects that are still holding back on monetization. One example is Joy, a service that has helped tens of thousands of couples organize their weddings. Joy postponed the start of monetization for a long time. Fortunately, now they are making revenue and experiencing rapid financial growth.

What Can Be Learned from This Case Study?

1. Investment in projects with high potential profitability can be justified even at the pre-monetization stage. In fact, startups generally tend to be unprofitable, especially in the early stages. You must learn to assess the likelihood and magnitude of the potential return.
2. A crisis-era caveat: during a crisis, projects that do not generate income and growth and do not have enough funds are forced to close or be sold for next to nothing. The exceptions are projects that receive the support of deep-pocket investors who are holding out for post-crisis growth.
3. If you have invested in a project that is postponing its monetization, be sure that it has a sustainable business model. If you aren't able to verify this in focus groups or with similar methods, at least check the numbers with Excel.

In the end, you can almost always find comparable projects and business models.

However, if a company waits too long to enter the market, we consider it a high-risk project.

2

THE AIRBNB AND TRIPACTIONS CASE STUDY

MORE GOLD, PLEASE, OR: A LITTLE GREED CAN SAVE THE WORLD

It has already been mentioned here that it is good not only to have money, but also to know how to use it wisely. Of course, these two abilities are not always found together. Startups that are supported by experienced investors carefully monitor their financial flows and have a financial director as one of the company's main managers. At later stages in the life of a business, a full-fledged financial services department takes shape.

Both emerging and established businesses face the problem of how much, when and from whom they should attract money at the next round. It is a headache common to all.

There are several built-in conflicts of interest here. Both founders and investors earn more when each new round comes infrequently and at a valuation many times higher than the previous ones. Debt financing can also be beneficial. Despite the pressure it puts on the cash flow, it does not lead to any dilution of equity. Therefore, we see how, at different stages, companies raise very significant funds to ensure growth and increase sustainability.

For example, consider TripActions, a travel management company for businesses and a relatively recent unicorn. After raising hundreds of millions of dollars in capital in the early rounds, the company received a half-billion dollar line of credit on the very eve of the pandemic shutdown. As a rule, credit lines are extended to companies with high turnover so they can finance possible cash shortages—that is, to ensure uninterrupted turnover. And if that turnover dries up, so does the line of credit. Now TripActions has turned to the market to obtain another loan, but this time a convertible one. That is, one where the debt can be repaid in shares during the next round.

Not everyone is lucky enough to enter a crisis in such a strong position. For example, the crisis in the travel market has forced one of the most outstanding unicorns, AirBnB, to raise convertible debt at a valuation significantly lower than the last time it sought funding. The company had planned to hold an IPO, but the pandemic altered those plans, causing it to use its financial cushion to merely survive and to preserve what is unquestionably a very fine business.

Unfortunately, not all companies are able to provide themselves with a financial umbrella in the face of an impending storm. One of my investment projects in the travel industry is a case in point. Investors loved this project so much that they drove up its valuation and ultimately invested in it. Six months ago, it held another round with a leading investor and there were no signs of coming troubles.

The situation changed very suddenly and dramatically, however, when a careful analysis showed that the growth rate was far behind projections. And the same investor, who had been prepared for an almost nine-figure round, proposed a new one in which the company was valued at a completely ridiculous amount—one so absurd that it's too embarrassing to repeat here.

In another, very recent example, we were the leading investor in Round A of an interesting travel startup. The company was growing wonderfully and then the black swan came to nest: a global pandemic. Literally, within a week, the business began to melt before our eyes; although its bottom line was fine. However, the threat of bankruptcy always looms when funds for ongoing payments dry up and you don't manage to muster them from internal reserves or raise them elsewhere because that whole process takes time. And this is exactly what happened. The company has had to go into reorganization until the market recovers.

You might wonder why all these examples are taken from the travel industry, especially because that is not our preferred line of business. Well, it just so happened that the latest crisis had the greatest effect on travel businesses that had not yet had time to build up hefty reserves or a strong enough reputation to ride out the difficulties.

But what has happened in industries that were spared from the brunt of the pandemic? The most successful ones have raised significant funds during the crisis, both for added stability and to maintain growth rates. One of our leading projects that works with the world's leading publishers unexpectedly asked its board of directors to approve debt financing. They did not do this simply to keep their pants on—they have enough money to weather even the worst of storms—but to help their business partners by making prepayments, thus strengthening those partners' competitive positions.

They do this with the following rationale: their partners are very influential global publishers, and making prepayments today enables you to consolidate relationships and obtain favorable terms tomorrow. This also precluded their competitors from doing the same thing. It's like buying luxury real estate in New York at incredible discounts.

Some companies attract funds to buy less fortunate competitors and other compromised assets. Projects that fail to achieve financial security in times of crisis are usually very accommodating. They might also have a great customer base, intellectual property or other undervalued assets. In such situations, 1 + 0 might equal not 1, but 10.

In such tough times, greed is not a vice at all, but a survival skill and a real competitive advantage. We investors also take advantage of the situation to gain access to dream projects. Startups that were self-sufficient yesterday are ready to accept financing for greater stability today.

What Can Be Learned from This Case Study?

1. Projects should maintain a balance that makes steady development possible. It is especially important to build up cash reserves so that in times of crisis or market opportunity you can maintain momentum and, if possible, strengthen your lead.

2. During a crisis, special attention should be given to projects in which leading investors are putting their money. These might become industry leaders after the market recovers.

3. It is critical that you run a stress test for all systems related to business processes. This guarantees not only that the project will survive, but also that you'll be able to turn a crisis into a window of new and amazing opportunities—a window that rarely opens, and that closes quickly.

3

THE AUTO GLASS GLUE CASE STUDY
ANOTHER LOOK AT FOCUS

I f I were asked to reduce the entire content of this book to a single word, it would undoubtedly be "focus." It would be good to repeat it every day to all the people in the venture capital industry—and it wouldn't hurt everybody else to hear it, either.

The projects that succeed not only remember their core competence, but also center all their efforts on it.

The fact is that as a startup develops, even the simplest idea and product can take on all sorts of functions and features— some important and some useless. But to avoid theorizing too much, let's look at concrete examples.

I was once invited to attend the presentation of a science startup backed by inventors and scientific executives. This company has set out to solve one of the burning questions facing mankind: what to do if tinted car windows have been banned but you really want them anyway?

After the authorities had introduced the ban on tinted windows, loads of substitute technologies had begun to appear, and this project offered still another. It turns out that car windows consist of two panes glued together, and that if you put additives in that glue (which was this company's know-how), you can darken the windows with an electric current.

Which business model do you think this startup adopted? Produce the additives? License the formula? You'll never guess!

They planned to produce car windows without knowing the first thing about the process or how to achieve market share. But the main question they failed to address was whether auto manufacturers even wanted such windows for their cars.

I advised the team not to stop with windows but to immediately start producing cars as well. After all, that market is larger and the company wouldn't have to negotiate for the purchase of their windows.

I was being facetious, of course.

This project had made the elementary error of taking the wrong approach. It is more common for startups to get this aspect right but to go wrong on positioning.

To avoid such mistakes, each project needs to answer the question: are we doing something new or improving on something that already exists? The answer—which is the project's main benefit to consumers—should serve as the basis of all subsequent steps. As the saying goes, "Every new idea is really a long-forgotten old one." From time to time, however, someone really does come up with a revolutionary new idea. Still, even if a startup comes up with something new, the real question is how it will influence the market. Is it a true breakthrough or just one more innovation in the world's growing sideshow of nifty inventions?

What's my point here? As a rule, whoever creates something so new that no one has seen or even imagined it before spends energy not only on promoting the idea but also on creating and educating the market.

Many new products did not connect with consumers for the simple reason that they appeared on the scene too early. One of the many examples of this is the Newton personal digital assistant (PDA). Launched by Apple, the Newton crashed and burned, whereas the iPhone released 10 years later by the same company literally changed the world. With the Newton, there was a typical misunderstanding between the market and the manufacturer. People did not understand who the intended user was of the Newton—a not-quite-pocket-sized computer-like device with handwriting recognition that cost a thousand bucks. The idea behind the product was definitely good, but it came at the wrong time.

If you are offering something new, you need to explain to the market what makes it unique and why consumers need it. Also, you need to be sure you aren't suffering from a false sense of novelty—maybe your examination of existing products was too cursory. Most people who claim that their product has no competition either failed to do the necessary research or have come up with some sort of rubbish that nobody wants or needs anyway.

And don't forget that if you have come up with something truly outstanding, you can be sure that your competitors—to whom you have already shown the way forward—are hot on your heels right now. For that reason, you need the help of clear messaging and accurate positioning to achieve the advantages that come to those who make the first move.

If, on the other hand, you are simply improving on a well-known operation, service or product, your market is clear—but it will be no less difficult to make a name for yourself in it. In this case, you need to think seriously about how your product differs from others and what specific benefit it offers consumers.

Tips on How to Do This:

1. Come up with a *killer feature* that will hook consumers. It must really be better than everything else, and you'll have to ensure that it not only stays that way, but also improves over time.
2. Position and promote your product in such a way that users clearly understand what you are offering and why it is better.
3. Important related functions to the main content of the product can be developed in-house. In this case, it isn't necessary to be the best of the best—excellent is good enough.
4. You should try to outsource all secondary functions. This is strictly an economic necessity because even if you manage to create several outstanding secondary functions, it will be very difficult and expensive to maintain leadership in all of them over the long term.
5. Create a team with a full set of competencies for implementing the main idea only. Outsource all the many remaining functions and skills, at least at the initial stage.
6. Don't lose focus. Choose one product or service and develop it to perfection. That is what "focus" means.

4

THE WEWORK CASE STUDY

DELUSIONS LOST, OR: IF A GROOM LOSES HIS
BRIDE TO ANOTHER MAN, HE MIGHT BE THE
LUCKIER OF THE TWO

The world is full of amazing and beautiful places that would be wonderful to visit. The dazzling views shown in ads and commercials excite your imagination, fueling your desire to leave at once to witness fairytale vistas, replete with picture-perfect glittering waterfalls and pink sand beaches. A friend tells you they are going with a group of people to one of these enchanting tropical destinations. Would you like to come? You think it over. You could afford it but the time doesn't feel right to spend so much money, especially when you don't know this group of people with whom you'd be sharing a vacation villa. You decide to pass, and as you scroll through social media, you see your friend flying first class to his island vacation and it stings a little.

It's much the same in the world of venture capital. Beautiful beaches and vistas beckon, promising an incredible journey. And yet, it doesn't work out for some reason. Should we grieve for the wonderful places we never visited and for the promising startups in which we never invested?

This case study is dedicated to such a trip that never happened and over which I have no regrets at all. I am speaking of WeWork, a much talked about project that was the first to come up with the idea of renting out office space for technology startups to share.

A remarkable thing occurs sometimes with investments—not often, but it happens. You look at a project, apply your time-tested criteria and decide...to pass on it. Yes, it looks very appealing, and yes, everyone is talking about it, but something stops you. Maybe the stars don't align in the form of a dollar sign, maybe you've worked with the founder before and seen exactly how they operate, or maybe it's just a hunch. It doesn't matter the reason or what you call it: what matters is that you decide to skip it.

Suppose the same founder unexpectedly comes to you with a completely new project and a great team and confidently states that they can do whatever it takes to succeed. You look at them and think, "What can these people do, really? Their previous project, a simple little thing, didn't get off the starting block, and now they suddenly want to conquer the world."

So you pass on it.

Then, the project miraculously begins to grow. You're watching and thinking, "There are signs of life, sure, but nothing amazing yet, and it's still a good thing I didn't invest in it."

The next time you look, the project has already taken off and is headed for the stratosphere. It's too late to climb on board, so all you can do now is wave goodbye.

Of course, all investors have their personal graveyards of missed opportunities. We discussed this earlier. On the other hand, though, there are many more projects and opportunities that they didn't miss. It helps if you repeat this mantra: "I have never lost money in a project in which I didn't invest." That makes everything a little easier and more fun.

When I first started angel investing, I focused on projects in Europe—and more specifically, in Austria. And I did so despite having 20 years of international business experience. Still, the time came when I had to expand my horizons. One day, I was speaking to a close friend of mine from New York who had also been investing in startups for many years. When I told him that I had decided to turn venture investing from a hobby into my full-time professional activity, he said, "Nice. When are you coming to New York? You should have a look at WeWork." I wrote off this strange grammatical construction—"look at we work"—as the result of a faulty connection. I couldn't understand why it was necessary to see how "they worked" over there.

Then, I flew to New York and visited the first-ever WeWork coworking space. It turned out that my friend was closely acquainted with the founder, Adam Neumann. When Neumann started the project, he turned to my friend for help, and my friend simply lent him a fairly large sum, without formally investing in the project.

The story continued the following year as the number of WeWork locations grew. We visited the first co-working space in San Francisco as well. A friend said to me, "Look at how WeWork is growing—and with no special technologies, either. They just rent a space, reconfigure it and lease it to startups and others at retail. Too bad I didn't invest when it was valued at $10 million. For the current round, its valuation stands at $500 million. What do you think, should I invest now?"

At the time, I was investing in projects valued at $1 million and $2 million, so even $5 million seemed like an astronomical figure. And the checks we wrote were of a corresponding size.

I considered the project grossly overvalued and told my friend. After all, we had already seen examples of similar companies such as Regus that still weren't demonstrating extraordinary dynamics. I didn't understand what made the WeWork business model so attractive and novel. To be honest, I didn't see the merit of its business model at all. And for such cases, I have a simple, tried-and-true rule: if I don't "get" the business model, I don't invest in the project.

Over the following years, WeWork became one of the most recognizable brands and a unicorn. The company was valued at more than $40 billion. Many of the teams I worked with had offices in WeWork premises. I even wound up working for a couple of years in one of their office spaces and was quite happy with it.

I had to work closely with WeWork when it bought the Israeli startup Unomy from our foundation. At the deal's close, WeWork offered us slightly better exit terms if we would take shares in the company instead of money. I knew WeWork was preparing an IPO, and this made the offer even more attractive.

I really liked the concept of WeWork, and I still think Adam Neumann is an interesting and capable entrepreneur. Sure, the numbers, the promises and the buzz augured well for tremendous financial success, but I understood the business model and assumed that the company's recent growth was driven by its questionable unit economics. Of course, I didn't foresee that it would take such a fall; I was just concerned about its overinflated valuation. As a result, I made the right choice and took the money.

After that, WeWork continued preparing for its IPO, but it never happened. When information about the IPO became public, potential investors began having similar doubts about the business model's sustainability. In short, the investment market did not react well and the IPO was postponed. The company's valuation plummeted and the founder was forced to leave the team.

What Can We Learn from This Case Study?

1. A business model can be highly scalable and temporarily soar, yet remain unworkable in the long run. Even seasoned investors can fall for a spectacular launch, but don't be fooled by all the hype.

2. A project's rapid growth does not free it from the need to constantly monitor such basic factors as unit economics. If a company only achieves growth by subsidizing demand, it will never be sustainable, and such stresses as a falling market, changing conditions or the emergence of strong competitors can lead to major difficulties and collapse.

3. Even a project that has scaled incredible heights early on might fail during a later stage. At every stage, it is necessary to track the project's status and dynamics and analyze threats and opportunities.

IN PLACE OF AN EPILOGUE

Few people read the epilogue, but it is a good idea to include one if for no other reason than it can refer to the many things that have happened during the writing of the book.

Because we live in a rapidly changing world, we must constantly adjust to new realities and try to imagine what tomorrow will bring. And this is true of our professional activities as well.

Attempts are now being made to bring artificial intelligence into the field of venture capital investment and the creation of startups, and there is certainly plenty of room for creativity in this regard. But until that becomes a reality, I hope the thoughts I have tried to convey in this volume will help you become a successful investor and/or entrepreneur.

We are all bound to make mistakes, but knowing someone else's experience can help us make fewer of them—and at a lower cost to ourselves and others.

Good luck!

www.ingramcontent.com/pod-product-compliance
Lightning Source LLC
Chambersburg PA
CBHW071604210326
41597CB00019B/3397